'Til Debt Do Us Part

Julie Ann Barnhill

HARVEST HOUSE™ PUBLISHERS

EUGENE, OREGON

Cover by Terry Dugan Design, Minneapolis, Minnesota

'TIL DEBT DO US PART
Copyright © 2002 by Julie Ann Barnhill
Published by Harvest House Publishers
Eugene, Oregon 97402

Library of Congress Cataloging-in-Publication Data
Barnhill, Julie Ann, 1965-
   'Til debt do us part / Julie Ann Barnhill.
      p. cm.
   Includes bibliographical references.
   ISBN 0-7369-0899-4
   1. Marriage—Economic aspects. 2. Marriage—Religious aspects—Christianity. 3. Married people—Finance, Personal. 4. Debt—Psychological aspects. I. Title.

HQ734 .B2497 2002
306.81—dc21
                                    2001059380

Printed in the United States of America

02 03 04 05 06 07 08 09 10 / VP-CF / 10 9 8 7 6 5 4 3 2 1

CONTENTS

Part Two: Chapter 13 Relief

To all the debtly sinners

True Confessions

Once upon a time I found the following items in my family's mailbox:

A) an "insufficient funds" notice in regard to my husband's and my joint checking account;

B) a handwritten note from a local business manager asking us, "What *are* your plans regarding the outstanding balance on this account?"; and

C) a note from my mother reminding me to pay the interest on a loan I had at my hometown bank. (Now really, should a 30-something mother of three need a note from her mother?)

Then, to top everything off, the interest check that I *had* already mailed was lost (honest to goodness) in the labyrinth of the U.S. Postal Service and landed—eight days after its due date in Missouri—in a PO box somewhere west of the Mississippi!

Okay, the payment was late and was incurring interest. I was also looking at an outstanding balance of nearly $1200 with a local business manager, and it wouldn't have surprised me a bit if our local banking officers had issued a warrant for my arrest.

My head felt like it was going to blow up, and I was ready to scream. Come to think of it, I did. I also cried and ranted and raved (the house was empty, the windows were closed), and I prayed—sort of. More of a spiritual lament, really. It sounded something like this:

> "God! I am so tired of all the financial stress in my marriage! I'm tired of juggling and shuffling and two-stepping. I'm tired of doing my best and failing! No matter how hard I try or how often I vow to get it right *this* pay period or *this* tax season, our marriage seems to be stuck in a financial waste-land. Rick says we 'just need more money,' but God, you know no matter how much or how little we have coming in month-to-month, it never seems to be enough! There has to be more to this problem than our just needing more money."

Disappearing Isn't the Answer

Sigh.

You too may be one of the thousands of Christian husbands and wives who—while knowing all sorts of money management do's and don'ts—still haven't been able to keep yourselves out of the monetary muck. And you may be one of many (including me) who—upon remembering those mistakes, pressures, and failures—find themselves wanting to run as far from the problems as possible. Disconnecting the phone, setting fire to the piles of envelopes in the mailbox, or faking my own demise and starting over in the Caribbean—well, they all sounded pretty good to me at one point or another.

And though I was tired of dealing with the fallout from my misdeeds, it was the condition of my heart that I most wanted to escape. Behind cliché quotes from the Bible and a clever façade of self-control and quasi-contentment beat the heart of a woman desperate to get and keep—regardless of the cost. I tried ignoring this reality—and found myself more than once just wanting to bail out on all things pertaining to money and marriage.

Unfortunately, people are doing just that. They are bailing in record numbers from the marital ship of "'til death do us part." Christians in particular. And if we're honest, it isn't all that shocking to those of us who have grown up in the post–baby boom generation. Statistics, percentiles, and the examples set before us in our own families and churches often reinforce what you and I already know: The relentless strain of financial worry—coupled with never-ending battles of wanting and "needing"—is perhaps the most lethal ingredient in marital conflict. All of this leads us, all too often, to separation and divorce.

Poor Souls

Here's the truth, pure and simple: I wrote this book for losers—bent, broken, and frustrated financial losers who've stopped purchasing money guides and attending high-priced seminars led by cheesy promoters (oftentimes "Christian" promoters) who promise health, wealth, and prosperity at every turn. (You will not read any "name it and claim it" miracle theology in the pages of this book. The *only* miracle involved with *'Til Debt Do Us Part* is that

I stopped worrying, shopping, or finagling long enough to get it written and that my husband Rick actually talked with me about his "feelings" regarding money!)

'Til Debt Do Us Part has been written with the authorities and experts in money *mis*management in mind—those poor souls suffering from undiagnosed symptoms of CFF (Chronic Financial Failure, discovered by yours truly). These pages have been written for anyone who has ever mutilated a checkbook statement, spent money they didn't have, and charged items on a credit card—just because they could! And it's for all the debtly sinners—too tired and too broke to wave a flag of surrender—who can muster up at best a garbled plea of "God, have mercy on a poor financial loser like me!"

Say What?

A loser?

You bet.

Loser: one who—as the Merriam-Webster dictionary so succinctly puts it—"loses especially consistently"! Indeed, I am one who has *especially consistently* found herself bewildered by the monetary mistakes she's made. One who has *especially consistently* squandered money and who has seen with her own eyes and felt with her own heart the painful consequences of such behavior.

Now, not only do I admit that I'm a loser—but I gloriously proclaim the truth of that reality. For it has only been through the discovery and confession of this status that I've been able to identify the issues affecting my finances and my marriage. More specifically, I've discovered *seven debtly sins* that have undermined my marriage as well as the integrity of my Christian faith. And they are at work in the lives of other men and women—perhaps in yours.

Perhaps you are a part of the silent contingent of financial losers—purchasing birthday items with an iffy-credit-line Visa and nervously waiting as automatic bank deposits post to your anemic checking accounts. When others speak of their savings accounts, perhaps you can think only of the Ziploc baggie tucked between the socks in your daughter's chest of drawers...it's her birthday cash and your answer to prayer on some occasions! In all likelihood you have a spotty record of tithing, your credit report reads "fair," and your marriage is teetering oh-so-precariously on the brink of disappointment.

Again and again I've talked with men and women at conferences and retreats as well as via e-mail, and over and over I've heard them say, "Can I ever relate to *that* debtly sin!"

- *Paula and Dave:* They're caught in a vicious cycle of kiting checks—shifting money from one account to the other, hoping to cover the never-ending demands of their creditors. Sometimes it works. Sometimes it doesn't. And all the while each one secretly resents the other's inability to manage money.

- *Melinda and Roger:* Paying an additional $7.95 a month for Caller ID service, they play a dangerous game of hide-and-go-seek with creditors. "Ignore them and they will go away" is their motto—and this works until the cheerless fall morning they watch as their 2001 Ford Expedition is ferried through their neighborhood behind a truck plastered with signs bearing, "They Owe, We Tow Repo Services Inc."

- *Allison:* Hiding purchase receipts from her husband, she's creating a mountain of denied debt.

- *Ben:* He's a CPA who earns his living managing other people's money, yet he ignores his own family budget and checkbook balance. *Karen:* His wife—who realizes one day she's tired of juggling it all by herself. So she leaves.

Make no mistake about it, debtly sins bankrupt marriages—emotionally, financially, spiritually, and physically. We don't want to be there—we don't want to fight, and we certainly don't want to be distanced from one another. But we are, and one of the root causes seems to be this issue of money and finances.

Money.

How we spend it. How we save it. Our tendency to never have enough (or never be content with what we do have).

Money.

What it can do. What it can't do. What it might do—if we only had some more.

Money.

The security it offers. The worries and fears its absence brings.

Money.

Is it always bad news?

Crazy Grace

Whatever the case with money itself, there is good news for you—you don't have to be a loser anymore! Your marriage doesn't have to end. Nor do you have to settle for "stuck, stuck, stuck" debtly matrimony. Contrary to what you may believe or may have been told, there is grace for people like you and me!

Take your time reading this book, and as you identify with the "been there, still am sometimes!" traumas, remember this: The goal is to get unstuck—and to do so while keeping the bigger picture of grace for financial misfits (that's you and me) in the forefront of your mind.

Listen to me, dear reader:

> No matter how much money you have spent or owe—
> *Never give in, never, never, never!*
>
> No matter how many lies you've spun to cover your mistakes—
> *Never give in, never, never, never!*
>
> No matter what relationships you've damaged or how much your reputation has suffered because of your lackluster financial acumen—
> *Never give in, never, never, never!*
>
> No matter what your present credit worthiness score is—
> *Never give in, never, never, never!*
>
> And no matter how enticing the prospect of abandoning your monetary problems and marriage may be—
> *Never give in, never, never, never!* [1]

'Til Debt Do Us Part is the written declaration and real-life testimony of one who has experienced God's redeeming grace and His incomprehensible patience and

love. It is His crazy, "in-your-face" grace that will enable you to say to yourself and to your frustrated spouse beside you, "I choose to *remain here* and experience the glorious grace that can transform each and every debtly sin that trips us up as man and wife."

God can and God will restore the relationships, the dreams, and yes, even some of the things that we have squandered through debtly sinning. He stands by, compelling us to "come to our senses" and to turn our hearts toward home. Just like the father that Jesus spoke of in Luke, chapter 15, your heavenly Father anxiously awaits you as you turn from your prodigal—wandering and reckless—financial ways. He watches as you take the first step toward Him.

And you know what? Not only will He welcome you with arms open wide, He will *run* to you—for He's been watching for you for a long time! And then, as He envelops you in the warmth of His embrace you'll hear Him whisper to your disheartened and bankrupt soul, "Welcome back, beloved, welcome back."

Author Brennan Manning sums it up most eloquently—

> God wants us back even more than we could possibly want to be back. We don't have to go into great detail about our sorrow. All we have to do, the parable says, is appear on the scene, and before we get a chance to run away again, the Father grabs us and pulls us into the banquet so we can't get away.[2]

All you and I have to do, dear financial loser, is show up.

You Might Be
a Financial Loser...

Before we plunge into debits and credits and do's and don'ts in earnest, let's put them aside for just a moment and take a humorous look at the symptoms of Chronic Financial Failure.

There's no particular science to this. It's just my belief that if you smile, grimace, or nod your head in agreement at three or more symptoms—well, welcome to the club and repeat after me: "My name is _____, and I am a financial loser."

- Upon your death you've instructed your spouse to burn the checkbook ledger and a) hope for the best, b) flee to Switzerland, or c) marry for money, and lots of it, the second time around.

- You have the following printed on the personal memo portion of the custom checks you purchased: "I won't think about that now, I'll think about that tomorrow. After all, tomorrow is another day."

- You've been arrested for forging Scarlett O'Hara's signature.

- You buy an item you don't need because the rebate makes it too good of a bargain to pass up, then never mail in the rebate.*

- Your retirement stock has taken so many dives, it could qualify for the Olympics.*

- The only "bond" you own is the one made by Elmer's Glue.*

- Your accountant sends you sympathy cards.*

- You ask a Girl Scout for a payment plan on your cookie order.*

- Your balance sheet has vertigo.*

- At your house, the tooth fairy leaves IOUs.*

- At the rate you're going you can retire at age 109 (or at least cut back to just your newspaper route).*

- You do more praying at the ATM than at church.*

- The salesclerk at Neiman Marcus has memorized your name, dress size, and credit card number.

- Your stack of bills is taller than your oldest child.

- The salesclerk asks you if you'd like a wheelbarrow to carry your purchases out to your car.

- You've moved out of state to avoid paying library fines.

- You paid more on late fees last year than you put in your savings (ouch!).

- You have a garage sale to help finance your Liz Claiborne purse purchase.

---

* Signs and symptoms courtesy of Martha Bolton, humorist and comedy writer extraordinaire.

- Your children hide their cash birthday gifts from you and your spouse.

- Your bologna has no first name.

- You give blood every day—just for the orange juice.

- McDonalds supplies you with all your kitchen condiments.

- Your idea of a 7-course meal is taking deep breaths outside a fine restaurant.

- Overdraft protection is the main criterion in selecting a bank for your joint checking account.

- You start your kids' college fund by purchasing Lotto tickets.

- You round, to the nearest *one hundred* dollars, the balance in your checking account.

- You balance your checkbook by standing on one leg.

- The check that you're expecting has already been spent.

- Buying something and "feeling good" go hand in hand.

- You hide receipts from yourself.

- You keep purchases bagged, tags intact, to return in case of cash-flow emergencies.

- Your accountant begins the meeting with, "The good news is you won't have any problems with capital-gains tax this year!"

- You can *still* identify with Veruca, the bad egg of *Willie Wonka and the Chocolate Factory* fame. You understand wanting things *now!*

- American Express calls and says, "Leave home without it!"
- You're formulating a plan to rob the food bank.
- You've rolled so many pennies, you've formed an emotional bond with Abe Lincoln.
- Long distance companies *don't* call you to switch.
- You rob Peter and then rob Paul.
- In a state-of-the-union address, the president thanks you for spurring economic growth.
- You've dropped, but yet you continue to shop.

How'd you do? Relax—you're in good company, and you've taken the first step in your road to debtly recovering—that of admitting your loser status. Just to make it official, let's repeat an oath and sign it in blood.

On second thought, let's just repeat the oath.

Financial Loser's Oath of Reality

I acknowledge that the state of my finances is a complete mess and is affecting my relationship with my spouse.

I acknowledge that without the supernatural work of God I will never be able to change my financial-loser ways.

I acknowledge that my debtly ways are controlling me.

I acknowledge that there are people who have been harmed as a result of my debtly ways and who I need to make amends to.

I acknowledge that finding and experiencing lasting change will be difficult.

I acknowledge that NOTHING is impossible with God.

PART ONE

Debtly Sins

Debtly Sin #1

Avoiding
Money & Marriage
Realities

1

Magnetic Personalities

Opposites attract.

It's as simple and as confounding as that. We learn in eighth-grade science that negatively charged electrons are drawn to positively charged protons. And it is that attraction of positive and negative energy that helps hold an atom together.

All the activities of this world depend on the dynamic tension of opposing forces. It can be as dramatic and scientific as atoms or as simplistically expressed as the "good guy versus bad guy" scenarios of books and movies. There is a basic push and pull of opposing forces that is active every moment within this incredible world of ours.

And think how boring life would be without them. Imagine ocean tides going out, never to return and lap again against a sandy shore. Can you conceive of Darth Vader with no Obi-Wan Kenobi? Or think of Shakespeare without the opposing forces of good and evil, free will and destiny, battling in the hearts and lives of Hamlet or Othello. It would be boring, I tell you, boring! Romeo and Juliet

would have *never* made it as a television movie of the week
if the parents of both characters had welcomed their bud-
ding relationship.

Opposites attract.

I have analyzed, read, surfed, and scanned countless
articles and journals discussing this dynamic of human
attraction. I've talked to experts and counselors, pastors
and lawyers, and with married couples on many occasions,
but no one has ever been able to give me a good *reason* why
this phenomenon occurs—it just does.

And that's the truth behind all money-and-marriage
realities—they just are.

Money & Marriage Reality: We Each Have Different Money Personalities

If you read a previous book of mine—*She's Gonna Blow!:
Real Help for Moms Dealing with Anger*—you will be
familiar with my interest in studying personality types. It
was while attempting to parent my second child (with
dismal results at that time I might add) that I began to
study the concept of temperament styles. What I learned
truly changed the manner in which I parented my children.

Now, you would assume I would translate all this temperament knowledge into the financial issues plaguing my
marriage. Assume nothing. In fact, I found myself becoming increasingly frustrated with the manner in which
Rick approached the subject of money. I just didn't get why
he had to have "x" amount of available funds in the
checking account to feel secure. I didn't understand why
he avoided bill-paying like it was a pile of underwear to be

sorted! And I could not, for the life of me, figure out how two people who slept together, had children together, and lived together could be such polar opposites when it came to rectangular pieces of paper with the words "In God We Trust" on them!

Rick and I were singing the classic Gershwin song "Let's Call the Whole Thing Off"—with a monetary lilt to the lyrics.

> You say save it and I say spend it,
> You say cash only and I say charge it;
> Save it, spend it, cash only, charge it,
> Let's call the whole thing off!

Why, oh why, did we seem to have such different opinions about money?

You've Got Style

Priscilla Evans Shirer, while speaking at a conference in Peoria, Illinois, gave one of the best illustrations of differing money personalities I've ever heard. I will leave it to you to attend a conference and hear for yourself all of Priscilla's dead-on conclusions about money and personalities, but here's a quick overview of what struck me so strongly.

One by one she covered the four basic styles—

1. the **D** personality—those who love to direct and want to see the bottom line in all things

2. the **I** personality—those who ply the people around them with humor, wit and a center-stage personality

3. the **S** personality—those who are steadfast and sensitive and are most likely to look out for your best interest

4. the **C** personality—those who appreciate (even demand) competence in all areas and see to the many details that the other three temperaments easily overlook

Priscilla then asked each group in the audience to stand and, one at a time, she proceeded to encourage others to— or warn them not to—borrow money from that specific personality type. I can tell you right now that my personality type is more prone to borrowing than giving, and there's a good chance I'll forget having done either one! Priscilla's great job of communicating the connection between personality and handling money that Saturday afternoon ultimately led me to consider the differing money personalities that Rick and I possess.

Money Roles in Marriage

Were Rick's and my different personalities contributing to—if not creating—many of the debtly issues in our marriage?

Psychotherapist Olivia Mellan, author of *Money Harmony: Resolving Money Conflicts in Your Life and Relationships,* says that it is normal for couples to assume opposite money roles. And these money roles naturally reflect your overall personality style—**D, I, S,** or **C.** Ms. Mellan lists six common role combinations that she believes most husbands and wives fall into:

1. a hoarder and a spender
2. a worrier and an avoider
3. a money monk and a money amasser
4. a planner and a dreamer
5. a risk-taker and a risk-avoider
6. a money merger and a money separatist[3]

If you're like me, you probably think you know which couple style you fit into, but before assuming any further, let's define the terms she uses.

- *hoarder:* budgets and saves carefully; hesitates over unplanned purchases
- *spender:* buys spontaneously and impulsively
- *worrier:* talks a lot about money; may be obsessed with it
- *avoider:* hates to deal with money at all
- *money monk:* thinks money is dirty and corrupting
- *money amasser:* self-worth depends on how much spent or saved
- *planner:* likes plotting finances in detail
- *dreamer:* a visionary who has dreams about the future but doesn't know how to get there
- *risk-taker:* loves adventurous investing
- *risk-avoider:* wants safe and secure investments and can't abide risk when making money
- *money merger:* doesn't want or need separate accounts
- *money separatist:* needs some or all accounts to be discrete

Whew! You can see why the money-and-marriage reality of money personalities is important to address.

Put a hoarder and a spender together for a holiday shopping trip—and stand back and watch the sparks fly!

Or imagine a planner wife married to a risk-taker husband—then watch their attempts in stock-market investing explode!

Worse yet, try to imagine a money worrier with a money avoider—one always expecting a less than ideal outcome; the other walking around with rose-colored glasses on and hands clamped over her ears, repeating "lalalalalalalalala…" (Can you guess which combination Rick and I represent?)

That Was Then, This Is Now

All sorts of emotional needs and frustrations can build up within a marital relationship when individual personality and its effect on our spending and money attitude aren't addressed!

Here's the frustrating thing. So often, the personality issues that become roadblocks to our communication and in our relationship as man and wife were at one time the very things that attracted us to one another. For instance, when Rick and I began dating I loved the fact that he listened to me. I mean *really* listened. He enjoyed my jokes, my stories, and my pontificating on a myriad of concerns and issues. And he loved the fact that I had huge dreams and aspirations for my future—which naturally spilled over into *our* future once we began talking of marriage. Rick loved my independence, and I loved the fact that he didn't try to tell me what to do. I loved the fact that Rick was laid-back, and I truly believed that I was going to attain all those noble dreams that I told him about.

Sometimes Opposites Annoy

Then we got married and along with the kids came money issues. And I found myself disliking Rick's reserved manner in dealing with life. I can remember one time in particular when my frustration level regarding money,

Rick, and our differing money personalities came to an ugly head.

I was the one talking to creditors and setting up a pay schedule with the local gas company. Rick told me he trusted me, and we both knew I was a better communicator. And though this may have been true, I still found myself resenting him for putting the responsibility upon me. So I did what any self-respecting I-personality wife would do…I gave him the cold shoulder. In and out of the bedroom.

Which naturally led to Rick having a few problems with my once-enchanting independent style. And while he didn't particularly comment on the cold-shoulder treatment outside the bedroom, he most certainly voiced his dissent regarding the other! In the midst of a heated conversation he suggested that the root cause for our money problems might be in my lousy (and still chilly) attitude toward him.

My "lead, follow, or get out of the way" attitude that Rick had so admired during our engagement was now more than a little annoying. And his quiet confidence in me no longer felt liberating, but stifling.

Remember When

Remember my illustration about atoms in the beginning of this chapter? Within the atom are protons and electrons—seeking each other out, positive to negative charge—completing what is necessary and lacking in the other.

I believe this phenomenon holds true to a large degree in humans also. We could call it the "atom effect"—opposite personalities or temperament types seek one another out in hopes of finding someone to complete them.

Rick tells me he was attracted first to my dark eyes and then to my outgoing and (admittedly) bombastic personality. His more mellow personality was drawn to—and more fully completed through—interaction with a dark-eyed comedian. I, on the other hand, was first attracted to Rick's Levi's 501 jeans, and I didn't really care what color his eyes were. Just as long as he looked as good in them as he did those Levi's—that was all I was thinking! But it didn't take long after meeting him till I found myself being drawn to his more selfless and self-deprecating manner.

I couldn't have expressed this to you those many years ago, but Rick was completing a part of me—not in a sexual manner, but rather in an indescribable manner of the soul. Being together just felt right, and I liked the way we were—together.

The truth is, Rick and I were both looking for someone to complete us. We were drawn to one another, and that powerful tug of opposites attracting has been a force in our relationship ever since.

Granted, it hasn't always been easy living with one another.

At times, we have abhorred the very differences that drew us together in the first place. I remember one time in particular when we were scheduled to attend a marriage retreat through a church we attended. I noticed that Rick was even less enthusiastic about going than he had been the year before.

So I began to talk and ask him questions—because that's what I do.

"Why don't you want to go?"

"Is there something wrong with us that you don't want to deal with?"

"What's your problem?"

I kept talking and talking, when finally he stopped me mid-inquisition and said, "That's why I don't want to go! You talk too much—and I never know what you're going to share when you open your mouth."

Well. I certainly understood that! So I told him I'd never open my mouth again and talk about our marriage. (However, I never ruled out becoming an author and writing all about us!)

Rick and I have both learned to adjust our expectations and to get this one thing through our thick, thick, stubborn skulls—we cannot realistically expect each other to change completely. I really do value Rick's quiet reserve and his ability to remain calm, cool, and collected in the midst of chaos. If he did turn 180 degrees and became just like me we'd be a mess!

And Rick has learned that my need to communicate and to be smack-dab in the middle of life is who I am. There's no way I can turn that part of me off, but I can honor him and keep his expectations in mind as I go forth and conquer! And just in case you've wondered, I check with Rick on all the stories and examples that I share about our marriage. He does have veto power. Unless I can talk him out of it.

Facing Facts

Take a moment and simply think about the way God has made your spouse. Consider their God-given temperament as well as the natural way they express themselves in certain situations.

How do they react when they feel threatened?

What is their first response when challenged to do something new?

Are they a risk-taker?

Do they worry about the weather tomorrow—or are they lucky if they notice a tornado bearing down on them in the spring?

One couple, who have been close friends of ours, now finish each other's sentences. She knows Bill like the back of her hand. And he knows what Beth will and will not do. Period. And though one will make an occasional comment that surprises the other, overall they *know* one another. They've learned how to read one another, and in this situation, they have learned to love one another with a greater depth and a richer passion because of that knowledge.

Rick knows I am never going to be a savvy saver by nature. Never. And I know that Rick will never be able to make a spur-of-the-moment purchase. Why, the very thought sends him into near cardiac arrest. (We are so opposite, it's scary!) The other night I told him, "I'm going to call around and get some quotes on having the driveway blacktopped."

No big deal, just a random act of thinking.

Sustained and pregnant pause—then a strained and painful comment from my spouse: "I don't think that's such a good idea."

But here's the good news. By the grace of God and with His help, we will continue to work our way toward a middle ground in the things mentioned above, as well as in countless other issues. We'll continue to grow up, and when we face a money-and-marriage reality we will have *already* purposed in our hearts to accept that quirk, that weakness.

For every money-and-marriage reality that has the power to destroy us as man and wife, there is financial grace and provision to strengthen us and to keep us keeping on.

2

The Crowded Altar

Everyone was in place.

The fidgeting flower girl now stood perfectly still—as well as the six bridesmaids to her side. Her ring-bearing counterpart, although making a spectacle of himself through nose-picking, remained right where his mother and the nervous bride (a.k.a. Aunt Dotty) had instructed him to stay. Both the bride's and the groom's side of the sanctuary were filled to capacity (to the relief of the groom's mother), and as strains of Debussy filled the room the handsome groom himself appeared in the company of his six closest friends. All eyes then turned to the church vestibule, where the bride was waiting for just the right cue.

Dum, dum, da-dum. Here comes the bride! As she grasped her bouquet her gaze was set straight ahead, and with each choreographed step she longed to catch a glimpse of the one who had won her heart. Then suddenly there she was. Grasping the hand of her beloved and feeling as though this moment and this time were theirs alone.

35

When you uttered the vows that made you man and wife, you too may have felt as though it was just you and your beloved standing before the altar of the church, or within the paneled office of a justice of the peace, or at the drive-through wedding counter in Las Vegas. But you were wrong. Allow me to introduce you to money-and-marriage reality number two.

Money & Marriage Reality: I Take Thee, Your Parents, and Your Dream Spouse

So you stood there in the presence of God and a multitude of witnesses, and you vowed,

"I take thee…"

Which of course you meant. You were pledging love and fidelity to the *one* man or woman standing before you. You were committing all you were and all you had to the *one* who had captured your heart and the *one* whom you wanted to spend the rest of your days with.

"It's just the two of us," one of you whispered. "Just you and me."

But is it? I hate to break into this Harlequin moment but, hmmm, I think we need a bit of reality about just who is in attendance at the altar of marital bliss.

More Than Two

There are in fact *eight* people standing there vowing "I do." *Eight* people standing before the bridesmaids and the fidgeting flower girl and her nose-picking sidekick.

"Thee" actually consists of eight people (at the very minimum!). And they are

- the actual bride and groom (2)
- the parents of said bride and groom (4)
- the man and the woman that the bride and groom *think* they're marrying (2)

Add them up—that's eight people standing at the altar! And long after the last toast has been made, the wedding gown cleaned and hermetically sealed, long after the honeymoon is but a distant bubble-bath memory of long ago—there will be *eight* voices chiming in on how one should handle the checkbook. Eight voices weighing the pros and cons of purchasing a 300-foot wide-screen TV. And eight voices lending their two cents' worth concerning the whys and whats of your money.

If you're a child of the '70s you'll know what I mean when I say, "Eight is enough!"

Monkey See, Monkey Do?

Propelling our actions and thoughts are patterns of behavior that we learned (both consciously and subconsciously) from our parents during our childhood and early adult years. Indeed, we are the sum total of various parts of our past. And that total adds up to some pretty interesting results in regard to money and marriage.

I once met a woman who told me that her husband's biggest fear in choosing a wife was that he would marry a woman who spent money just like his mother. His natural "money worrier" personality was intent on finding a girl whom he could count on not to break the bank. Lucky for him, the woman he pledged "I do" to erred on the side of hoarding rather than spending, and the financial aspects of their marriage have been relatively trouble-free. However, had he married someone more like me—well, I'm sure we probably would have had to work through a lot of "mother" issues during marital counseling!

Another couple I know discussed in great length the concern that the groom's family had regarding his bride's family's financial history. They were both born and raised in the same rural community where everyone knew everyone's business. "Business"—as in how often you pay your electric bill late; "business"—regarding how many pickup games of pool you put your money down for at the town center.

But more than that, in such a place everyone knows (or thinks they do) whether your word means anything in the grand scheme of things.

Well, the bride's parents had flunked the "business" test over and over again. They weren't exactly known for their exemplary attention to the financial details of life. Therefore it was with trepidation that the groom's parents listened as he announced his intention to go into business with his father-in-law.

"They just didn't think he could be trusted," my friend told me. "And I guess I can see their point. But I knew this was something that we could do together, and I knew that I could be just the shot of financial grace my father-in-law needed in order to do things right for once." He shook his head and then added, "The only problem was, my folks just wouldn't let that worry go. They bugged my wife about things, and frankly, their unwanted opinions and observations hurt my relationship with her and simply added more stress to the already stressful situation of beginning a new business."

Clichéd Truth?

There's an old saying: "The apple doesn't fall far from the tree." And though I would never say that you are destined to be just like your mom or dad, the fact is, we establish a lot of lifelong patterns based on their examples—be they good or bad.

Money—how was it handled in your family of origin? Physically, did your mother or father handle cash, checks, credit cards, or money orders? How about the emotional aspects of money in your childhood home? Did your parents discuss money in a positive way in your presence? Or was arguing the most frequent mode of communication?

If your parents did fight about money, do you remember feeling insecure? Did you worry about your ability to have shoes, clothing? Perhaps you were raised by a single parent—were there times when the resources to attend school functions and participate in extracurricular activities were simply out of reach?

Maybe your mother or father never mentioned money. Nothing said one way or the other about having enough or too little. If there was a problem or an argument concerning finances perhaps you were never aware of it—but maybe, just maybe, there was an undercurrent of tension that you somehow knew was there.

And I guess it's quite possible that some other husbands or wives struggling with CFF could have grown up never hearing "We can't afford that," "You don't need that," or "No."

Financial Backgrounds

That's more the background I came from.

I was adopted at age three by a couple nearing their 40s. Both my mom and dad worked full-time, and they were thrilled to have a child to adore and lavish their affection, time, and monetary blessings upon. I was an only child—as was my adoptive father—so when Christmas came around, let me tell you, it was one big blowout! There were gifts galore as well as an extravagant outpouring of emotional security and belonging. When I was young (from ages seven to ten) I truly believed my parents were millionaires.

Now, Rick came from a completely different background.

He was one of four children, and his mother did not work outside the home. Rick's father earned an honest day's wage in the heart of central Illinois, at Caterpillar, Inc. However, during the 1970s and early 1980s Rick's father found himself walking a picket line as well as living on unemployment benefits during company layoffs.

Rick was loved, but unlike me he often heard the words "We can't afford that." Where I grew up constantly asking for things and receiving cleverly wrapped presents on Valentine's Day, Independence Day, and even St. Patrick's Day, Rick knew to anticipate gifts only on birthdays and at Christmas.

Up until age 20, Rick had traveled to two states outside Illinois.

I, on the other hand, had visited numerous states on family vacations and had participated in a student ambassador program to Europe as a 15-year-old. While I was eating gyros and walking the boardwalk near the salty aqua waves of the Aegean Sea, Rick was washing a never-ending stack of dishes at an Italian restaurant and saving every dollar he earned.

Rick and I couldn't have come from more opposite financial backgrounds! And *that* reality has reared its ugly head on more than one occasion.

What We Have Here Is a Failure to Communicate

One of the languages mentioned in Dr. Gary Chapman's book *The Five Love Languages* is the language of gifts. Gifts as in presents, baubles, knickknacks, and sundry items.

Now, my family spoke the love language of gifts! Each birthday was met with carefully wrapped presents. If someone accomplished something special a present was given in celebration. My mother routinely sent flower arrangements to my grade school teachers on Valentine's, Christmas, and Easter. And though I didn't particularly appreciate her gesture after grade four, I knew that she was just expressing her thanks in a very tangible and "gifty" manner.

My parents, as well as my grandmother, had always communicated their love for others and me in the language of gifts.

This is when it started to get dicey. For you see, the love language that Rick's family spoke was that of quality time spent with one another. Rick grew up attending fish fries, cookouts, and baseball events with aunts, uncles, and cousins galore. Food and family were big events and were key in expressing love for one another within the Barnhill family. Rick has wonderful memories of the stories and laughter that arose from these gatherings. And that's all well and fine—with one possible exception.

He was completely illiterate in the love language of gifts (which is the lovespeak I most want to hear)!

So when my birthday rolled around, I expected him to speak with a nice big expression of his *amore*—all wrapped up in a large box with sparkling wrapping paper.

I got a card.

When our first baby was born, I expected an expression of his love and appreciation for my having survived the feat of childbirth preferably draped around my neck or adorning my finger.

He *told* me, "I love you."

I told him he was a terrible husband! And so it continued. It wasn't long before I was steaming weeks before any significant event (Valentine's, Mother's Day, Groundhog Day), and all the while Rick remained illiterate!

Now You're Talking My Language!

Some of our most traumatic money-and-marriage moments have centered on Rick's inability to speak the language I grew up hearing—that language of giving and gifts that expressed to me a sense of belonging, importance, and love. Lest you think me completely self-centered, I too have had to own up to love language realities. Rick speaks a different one than I do, and he also senses love, belonging, and importance through it.

Even though the fact that Rick considers *time spent together* as a gift in and of itself doesn't compute in my stuff-luvin' brain, I was still able to experience an incredible demonstration of this language during the writing of this book. Thanks to the generous offer of a friend living in Colorado, Rick and I were going to spend a romantic weekend in a Rocky Mountain getaway. I had flown out several days before on business and was looking forward to having time alone with my husband. I had saved a little fun money, and we planned on skiing and taking in the sights at Breckenridge and Copper Mountain.

Then, two days before Rick was to fly out to Denver, someone stole the money I had tucked away in my billfold. My credit card was still there, but that lone Visa was maxed out with airfare and car-rental charges.

All thoughts of an enjoyable weekend flew way as I calculated doing a mountain resort in Colorado on 30 dollars. (For some reason the thief did leave a ten and a twenty. Guess he figured it would pay my shuttle ride back to Denver International Airport!) I just knew the weekend would be a complete bust—and I resigned myself to three days spent arguing with Rick as to how I could have gotten myself in the mess to begin with.

But boy, was I wrong! And did I ever get a lesson on speaking Rick's love language!

First, some benevolent friends in Denver presented me with the exact amount of cash that had been stolen. I cried as they handed it to me, and I began to believe that it was possible for us to have a decent time after all. Now we had money to spend. We could buy stuff. Buy ski tickets. Pick up gifts for the kids and eat.

But here's the kicker. After all that worry about the cash that was stolen and after all the mental gymnastics over how we could possibly enjoy ourselves with so little fun money—we actually spent very little.

But emotionally, we broke the bank.

At Rick's request, all we did (well, sorta) was talk, hold hands, drive through the mountains, and simply hang out with one another. I know it sounds dorky, especially to those of you living in the Rocky Mountains who are used to seeing snowcapped peaks shimmering in the noonday sun, but we simply took in the grandeur of the scenery and the joy of simply being with one another. This was the first time in my married life that I had *ever* not spent money on anything—except for food and bubble bath.

Here's the deal. Rick's love language is expressed through time spent together and sharing a plate of tasty Southwestern food on the side. And while I was figuring up the cost of ski-lift tickets and renting equipment, all he wanted to do those few days together was to "be" together and show me that he loved me.

"Dream Spouse"?

Despite the fact that Rick and I have known each other for more than 18 years, I still find it hard to believe that he wants to be with me.

Me. A woman who can be quite moody and impossibly hard to please.

Me. A woman who's gained the proverbial marriage weight and who's misplaced more money than she cares to remember.

Me.

Here's what I think. Sometimes it's not the "dream spouse" your husband or wife had in mind that's so difficult to live up to—but rather the "dream spouse" that *you* thought *you* were going to be.

When I stood before all our friends and family on that cold December evening in 1987, I wanted to be the wife of Rick's dreams.

I was going to be a chef in the kitchen.

A vixen in the bedroom.

And—well, though I didn't give it a lot of thought, I certainly didn't want to be a complete financial failure with our earnings and investments.

I've disappointed myself over and over again.

Let It Go

The humbling truth is this. I cannot—and no one is really asking me to—live up to all the things I thought I'd be. Nor can Rick live up to all the things he thought he'd be. And perhaps a few of us reading the pages of this book simply need to let go of the fantasy bride or groom that was standing next to them at the altar.

That groom who was going to meet all your emotional needs?

Let him go.

The bride who was going to do things your way without fail?

Definitely let her go.

Visions of never messing things up?

Let them go.

Guilt from never meeting your ideal as a husband or wife?

Let it go!

I know this is extremely difficult. But if we want to be successful in the dynamic give-and-go of marriage, it is absolutely imperative. And here's some good news. You don't have to do it alone! In fact, you're crazy if you think you can do it all by yourself.

No, you're going to need the power of One who knows you—the One who knows your love language, your money personality, and every other minute detail—because He Himself formed you! If we're ever going to "let it go," we will first have to surrender and call upon the One—Christ Jesus, our Lord—for strength and lasting change.

3

The Last Taboo

I took a random survey of married men and women and asked them the following: "Given these choices, which would you *least* prefer to do?"

A) Dance naked on a tabletop at the nearest Denny's while yodeling "The Star Spangled Banner"

B) Bungee-jump from a one-story building

C) Discuss your current financial situation and earnings-to-debt ratio with an author friend*

I don't think my friends are alone on this one. Truth be told, most of us would rather talk about anything than our financial-loser status.

A few years ago, a friend—*former* friend—looked at an old driver's license photo of mine and commented—

"Whew! You were a big gal, weren't ya!"

---

* The wise reader would refrain from visiting the local Denny's and avoid walking beneath one-story window ledges!

I was stunned! I was dumbfounded! I couldn't believe he had said that! But a few months after that another friend topped even him. This one asked in all sincerity and with full expectation of an answer, "So, Julie, how much money are you making, now that you're writing books?"

Say what? Give me Denny's or give me death!

Forget about the topic of sex being taboo. I'll tell you what is—*discussing money matters*—be they good or bad, in the black or swimming in red!

There's just something about actually verbalizing your financial inadequacies that strikes fear in the hearts of the bravest souls. *Admitting* your ineptness and debtly ways with money, credit cards, retirement planning, or financial goal-setting can leave you feeling more than a little ashamed, embarrassed, and looking for the nearest hole to dive into for cover!

Those who speak confidently in public (me, for instance)—those who wing their way through life—become strangely silent when sitting face-to-face with a mortgage officer. And ordinary men and women all over creation tremble at the thought of discussing their true financial situation with the one they "I do'd" so many years ago.

I'd Rather Be Yodeling

I confess. We confess!

We have painted ourselves into some very tight and hard-to-navigate corners. Years of debtly choices have left their mark on our relationship. And discussing and rehashing those realities with one another—let alone the readers of this book—has been more than a bit intimidating.

But you see, that's a big part of the entire financial taboo in marriage. The truth is, it is very, very, *very* intimidating to confess these vulnerabilities and weaknesses to one another. We may say we desire intimacy in our marriage relationship, but often when that particular level of intimacy comes wrapped in the form of a broken and defeated spouse, we find ourselves oddly repulsed.

Like it or not, I think many of us as husbands or wives simply want to have our cake and eat it too.

We want intimacy—but not to the level of reality that it sometimes takes us.

We want a vulnerable spouse—but not *too* vulnerable.

Let me share a painful example.

More Than I Wanted

It was 1996, and after ten years of retail management, Rick was ready for something new. Actually, he had tired of it about three years before, but the thought of leaving what was sure and comfortable was more than a bit intimidating. Factors such as my wanting to continue to stay at home with our youngest son, Patrick, and Patrick's continued medical expenses because of asthma and other respiratory illnesses, fell like a weight on Rick's shoulders.

Rick was in fact stuck.

Stuck—in a job he didn't particularly enjoy.

Stuck—with "male" responsibilities screaming at him at every turn.

Stuck (though he never said anything out loud)—with a wife who had put a lot of pressure on him to climb the ladder of success, to earn a higher income, and to achieve a measure of recognition within his corporate field.

I watched him during those years and, believe you me, his body language screamed "stuck"!

Morning after early morning he would sit on the edge of our bed, his shoulders hunched and his head bowed. Tired before his 14-hour day had even begun. And his eyes! They spoke volumes.

"I want something different." "I'm tired of doing what I've been doing." "I'm dancing as fast as I can…and I *hate* dancing!"

Now you should know something here. I had pressed Rick over the years to be absolutely honest and open with me. *Pressed*—buying countless books on the subject of communication, marriage, and trust, and placing them strategically throughout the house. *Pressed*—trying to get him (forcing him, more like it) to engage in meaningful conversations concerning his dreams for his future and our family. *Pressed*—going on and on about his need to discover his vocational "passion" and to be willing to take risks when he'd figured it out.

Man—no pressure, huh?

Then one day Rick took me up on all those *pressing* offers. And boy howdy, did he ever "share."

"Julie, I don't know what my 'passion' is! I don't have time to think about that. I get up every morning before the sun rises, I take a shower, I get dressed, eat some cereal, go to work, do my job, come home, eat dinner, and maybe catch a TV show or two." He paused, took a breath, and added with a note of sarcasm, "And then I get to go to bed, wake up, and do it all over again.

"Meanwhile"—by this point he was in full "communication" mode—"you're home and all you can seem to think about is why I don't 'love' my job more, or wonder why I don't have a passion for life.

"Well, I'll tell you why, Julie—I'm tired.

"Tired of setting up Christmas merchandise in September.

"Tired of shelving chocolates, plastic bunnies, and green plastic grass and tired of hardly ever seeing a cross or a nod to the true meaning of Easter and every other holiday that actually means something to me.

"Tired of dealing with grown women who act like seventh-grade junior high students.

"Tired of working 50- or 60-hour weeks, only to get my check and see it all disappear in a matter of hours."

Then came the coup de grace. "I can't be all these things you want, Julie, and I'm not going to make the money you so want me to....if you want those things, well, you're going to have to go back to work."

You Asked For It

Well, Rick dared to drop his cloak of self-sufficiency and "shared" after all. But it wasn't quite what I had imagined. So I responded in the manner fit for my personality type.

I panicked.

Yep—panicked.

Something may have been lost in the translation because all I heard was this: "I'm going to quit my job, sit in the La-Z-Boy, watch Andy Griffith, and make you leave Patrick [one year old] and go get a job!"

Stop the train! I may have said I wanted him to "share" his fears, to be more open and vulnerable. Pooh—I may have even wanted him to admit a weakness or two! But this...uh, I don't think so!

My mind raced with questions:

Does he expect me to leave Patrick with a baby-sitter and work now?

Has he resented my stay-at-home status all these years?

And considering how much control and effort it must take to suppress these emotions—do I even know who this man is?

I was absolutely stunned and sat before him speechless. (Now you know it was serious!)

Going Through the Motions

Here's what I think.

We may say we want our mate to confess worries, doubts, failures, and fears regarding the financial aspects of life and marriage. And may truly believe we mean it. But for many of us, when we glimpse our husband or wife "there"—unguarded and weak—we find it more than a bit disconcerting, and even a bit repulsive.

And why would that be? I submit that oftentimes we are simply role-playing our parts in this mysterious relationship called marriage. We come to the altar with all sorts of expectations, and we refuse to admit when they are in fact unrealistic and unattainable. I submit that too many of us as husbands and wives are simply going through the motions of intimacy—often allowing our sexual union to compensate for the lack of emotional and verbal intimacy we engage one another in.

Face it. It probably *is* easier to dance on a tabletop naked and yodeling than to open ourselves up to the truly intimate union of sharing in one another's weaknesses. It's not a safe place to go. Yet, until we do…we will continue to stumble and continue to miss the mark of true intimacy that every human heart cries out for.

Debtly Sin #2
Unrealistic Expectations

4

Once Upon a Marriage

Fairy tales often begin with the same basic ingredients.
A prince, a princess, and some sort of wicked influence that threatens their attaining happily-ever-after status. So far be it from me to change the fairy-tale rules of engagement.

In a time not so very long ago (1987), in the kingdom of Hannibal, Missouri, there lived a handsome prince named Rick Barnhill and a princess bride named Julie. The prince ruled in the province of Wal-Mart, where he thwarted the evil plans of shoplifters in zone five shopping aisles.

The princess traveled in her royal coach (sporty two-door Chevy Monza Spyder) to the kingdom of Palmyra, Missouri, where she taught a classroom of spirited fourth-graders and learned the value of double-checking her subtraction math facts for gifted students.

The newly betrothed prince and princess spent their days and nights dreaming of what lay ahead. Visions of a belated honeymoon in Cancún danced in their heads. The princess worked on losing 25 pounds in preparation for the sand beaches and lazy afternoons of swinging from a shady hammock—whilst the prince attempted to secure a reservation at a resort specializing in heart-shaped Jacuzzis.

Indeed! The prince and princess were intent on living the good life that they had talked about during their four years of college dating. They were convinced, with 20-something bliss, that nothing could deter them from achieving the marital image that *Bride's* magazine promised. They were young, and the world was theirs for the taking.

Then, ugh…the beautiful princess felt royally sick. And the insensitive prince told her she didn't look so great either.

She felt puffy.

She became very irritable and sundry "glands" became incredibly tender. Night after night she retired *alone* to bed (7 P.M.) to awaken a few short hours later (7 A.M.).

I wonder if I'm…? the heaving princess thought one of those mornings while studying the bowl of her porcelain throne. She journeyed to a retail store and purchased a modern miracle.

Three drops.

Five minutes.

And two blue dots later, the happy, elated, flabbergasted, and joyous princess shared the news with her heart-shaped-tub-lovin' spouse.

"You couldn't possibly be," he said.

"Just connect the dots, dear," the princess replied, and she handed the clueless prince the test stick. After a second, third, and fourth look the ashen-faced prince replied, "Well, I'll be"—and passed out.

The princess threw up one last time and went to bed.

Surprise! Surprise!

I'm sure this will come as a great shock to you, but Rick and I never did make it to Cancún, Mexico. Nor did I lose the 25 pounds that were going to help me fit into a two-piece bikini for the first time in over a decade. And the heart-shaped tub thing? Well, we're 15 years down the road, and that still hasn't happened!

A lot of things changed that fateful evening when we learned we were joining the Elvis and Priscilla Presley Honeymoon Baby Club. Vacation saving gave way to a crib purchase, and the sexy swimsuit turned into a nursing bra and cotton briefs. Suddenly Rick wasn't only my husband but—gasp!—the father of our child. And that meant I was a mother.

Umm, this was one "expectation" I was not expecting to expect!

More Fairy Tales

We all come to the altar with ridiculously lofty expectations.

Now, I don't think it's the worst thing on the face of the earth to have expectations about one another. After all, how awful it would be if you looked through your bridal veil to the one you're pledging your life to and thought, *Nope, I expect nothing from this man, absolutely nothing.*

It's good to expect something—we just seem to have a difficult time keeping it reasonable!

It's time for another confession. I was packing a serious load of expectations regarding any future husband of mine. I expected him to

1. demonstrate the masculine tenderness of Pa Ingalls of *Little House on the Prairie*

2. amass the wealth of Ted Turner

3. articulate the spiritual wisdom of Billy Graham

4. display the spiritual looks of Carmen

5. entertain me with the humor and wit of Billy Crystal

And it's not like Rick didn't have expectations either. He expected his wife to be Demi Moore. Clearly we both were just a little off balance in our expectations for a future spouse—though I find Rick's to be particularly unrealistic and shallow.

After all, humans always expect something from or of each other. Whether we are consciously aware of them or whether they play softly amid the background noise of our minds, our expectations come into play in the arena of money and marriage. Unrealistic expectations can bring a plethora of stress-related issues to our marriages: misunderstandings, communication breakdowns, distrust, and heated arguments, to name a few.

Let me share with you a few debtly expectations that we and many other couples have struggled with. Any initial premise that these expectations were somehow realistic and attainable quickly hit the wall of reality once the wedding vows were exchanged!

Unrealistic Expectation #1:
Our Marriage Will Always Be Marked by Romance

Ever notice that in the land of soap operas no one's husband ever heads to the bathroom with the Sunday sports section tucked underneath his arm? Have you ever seen Erica Kane balancing her checkbook? Or answering a telemarketing call at a quarter to ten in the evening? And I'll tell you the chief far-fetched and unrealistic expectation that soap operas and their ilk breed in the hearts of women everywhere.

That of the "Romantic Bathtub Rendezvous."

Just imagine (because, trust me, it will not happen on a regular basis in your world!) 3972 glowing candles casually placed—yet with studied attention to mood lighting—around a bathtub the size of Rhode Island filled with sexy bubbles. The fantasy—or expectation—is of your husband joining you in an evening of passion and good clean fun.

But, come on, you and I both know that this is a *fan-ta-see!* It's just not going to happen for most of us couples. And we all know why. The average couple couldn't sit in their bathtub if they wanted to!

First, you would have to remove the collected soap scum from the past five months. Once this was accomplished and after the pungent aroma of the green-colored disinfectant had dissipated, you would then need to remove the plastic shark, Play School fireman, one-legged naked Barbie, 16 Matchbox vehicles, bacteria-infested spongy thing that the 4-year-old refuses to part with, and 11 trial-size Bath & Body Shop containers—courtesy of your 14-year-old daughter.

Then and only then could you attempt to find a piece of soap that hadn't been sitting in its own "soap juice" for the past seven weeks! Ugh. And we wonder why the romance factor begins to fizzle!

Truth be told, marriage is often anything but romantic.

Just ask any couple who find themselves synchronizing their Palm Pilots to schedule time for romantic interludes.

Trying to find time for—scheduling, no less—sexual encounters with one's spouse can become quite disheartening to the romantic soul. Add to that financial difficulties, and the expectation of song and romance can quickly turn sour!

Unrealistic Expectation #2: My Spouse Will Make Me Happy

Wrong.

Not going to happen.

Incorrect.

Misinformed.

Keep dreaming.

I've got a great piece of real estate for you in the *Arizona* Everglades.

No one can *make* us happy. Oh, they can influence our attitudes and encourage us one way or another, but "*make* you happy"? Mark it down, this won't happen...at least for the long haul it won't.

And the long haul is exactly what we're striving for in this thing called marriage.

If you're sitting around waiting for him or her to push just the right button or say just the right things or buy just the right gifts to propel you into a cosmos of happiness... well, you're going to be waiting a mighty long time.

And this expectation leads quite nicely into unrealistic expectation #3.

Unrealistic Expectation #3: My Spouse Will "Just Know" What I Need

If your spouse has joined the local psychics' union maybe.

Other than that one remote—and completely spurious—possibility, you'd better count on this expectation biting the dust of reality pretty quickly. I mean, really—I don't know what *I* want half the time! How on earth am I supposed to "just know" all *his* wants, desires, and needs?

On second thought, I probably *can* sum up all his (and 99 percent of the male species') basic wants, desires, and needs! Better yet, I'll let author Dave Meurer do that for me, as he does in his hilarious book *Daze of Our Wives: A Semi-Helpful Guide to Marital Bliss.*

> Running the men's ministry carried with it the task of setting a theme for the annual men's retreat. I chose "real life" as the topic, not only because I wanted to discuss serious issues that men face in the "real world" but also because this theme is so broad I could cram just about anything into it at the last minute, thus allowing me to procrastinate until the last possible second (which I did).
>
> Someone else was in charge of music, and we ended up singing a little verse that goes, "He's all I need, He's all I need, Jesus is all I need." You just repeat it a few times and it turns into a song.
>
> As we were singing, this little chorus brought back memories of a conversation I had had several years earlier with my two sons, Mark and Brad. We were in church, singing, "He's all I need, He's all I need, Jesus is all I need," when Brad, then eight, leaned over and pointed out, "You need air too."
>
> "And water," chimed in Mark. "You can only go about two days before you die." So I conveyed this story to the guys at the retreat.

"My kids were right, really," I said. "But the list of necessities doesn't stop at air and water. Frankly, I'd kind of like to work sex into the mix. This is not easy to do in a song."

Guys emitted stifled, nervous laughter and cast quick looks around the room while I jotted some words on an overhead transparency.

I then laid a song sheet on the projector, and we all sang, in thunderously loud voices:

> He's all I need, He's all I need, Jesus and air and water and a decent Italian restaurant and sex, is all I need.

The guys REALLY liked this song. They wanted it in the hymnal.[4]

I rest my case.

Now, we ladies on the other hand are a bit more high-maintenance. And many, if not all, of us truly do expect our menfolk to read our minds and know the exact thing to say or do, or as can often be the case, know what *not* to say!

For instance, when I tell Rick I need to go out for dinner with him I pretty much expect him to "know" that I'm really wanting companionship. Despite what he may believe, I'm really not thinking up ways to spend money… rather, I am trying to express my need for relationship with him.

He often fails this "just know" test.

The truth is…no one can read our minds. And even when we've met our spouse's need—the Dave Meurer "water, air, sex, and food" requirement or the three-course-dinner estrogen need—there's a good chance we both have untapped wants, still waiting to be discovered.

Unrealistic Expectation #4:
We Won't Make Mistakes Like Our Parents

Trust me, let this one go—quickly!

Because you will—make mistakes that is. In fact, you'll probably mess things up worse than they did in many regards. And boy, won't that be embarrassing when you have to take back every "I'm never gonna!" threat you uttered against them?

You see, the goal isn't to get married just so you can "one-up" your mom or dad. Nor should we embrace the unrealistic expectation that our lives are meant to highlight with a glaring yellow marker all the financial mistakes they made. Rather, we should actually learn from the mistakes and debtly sins and errors that they committed and then apply them to our own ups and downs as man and wife.

Lesson Learned

I've told my parents many times since becoming a parent myself, "You should have told me 'No' more and you should have said, 'You don't need that,' much more often than you did."

As I confessed previously, I grew up "expecting" things. And I recall that seldom, if ever, did I hear my mother specifically say, "Julie Ann, I would like to have something new for once. You can wait."

Just for the record, I was a pretty grateful kid. And I think all my past and being an older adoptive child had something to do with that. Lest you fear, I was never quite as spoiled as the bad-egg character named Veruca in the classic movie *Willie Wonka and the Chocolate Factory*. I didn't cross my arms, puff out my chest, and spit verbal daggers at my parents. (Good ol' Dad would have dealt soundly with that, believe me!)

I was a good egg. But one who expected far, far too much!

So, fast-forward 20 years, and we find Julie Ann the mother of a daughter herself.

Much to Kristen's chagrin, I have learned a lesson or two from my spoiled past, and am even now attempting to teach her the value of the money her father and I earn! Just as I was kissing her good-night the other day, she requested that I purchase tickets for a concert by a popular music group that will be in our area.

"How much are the tickets?" I asked cluelessly.

"Only $48 apiece," she replied without blinking an eye.

"Only"! Only $48 a ticket for a concert! Zoinks! I'm not sure she's taking so well to this "appreciating our money" lesson after all!

Up until your mid-to-late 30s, you truly believe you can walk unscathed through the land mines of marriage. With enough education, enough love, enough attention to detail, you can avoid them all.

Ha! Then, with each successive white hair that spoings from your chin, you realize…it was all a fantasy. The bells go off and you truly get it!—

We're going to mess up too.

No matter how we try not to.

No matter what our portfolio earnings are or what our IPO statement says. No matter what we tell our friends our children have learned. Nope—we will mess up in this area of life too!

So I've decided to cut my parents some slack. How 'bout you?

Something Better Will Come

I can promise you this: Every *unrealistic* expectation will hit the wall of marital and financial reality. It may happen two months after "I do," or two decades, but make no mistake about it—those expectations will bite the dust!

So I propose the following. Instead of clinging madly to these crazy expectations and waiting like Chicken Little for the sky to fall, let's just face up to them, open our clenched fists, and release them. Just like that.

Let's let them go, and let's glory in our spouse and our marriage just as they are. Let's let go of the happily-ever-after fantasies that derail our love for one another. Let's let go of the faultfinding that always accompanies our unmet expectations. Let's let them all go—and fill the empty places their vacancy brings with grace.

5

Fractured Fairy Tales

One of my favorite movies, and one with some great quotes—if not the best cinema quotes of all time—is *The Princess Bride*. If you've not watched this modern classic, run to your nearest video store, grab your spouse, and sit down and enjoy the entertainment!

In a hilariously skewed and offbeat kingdom of Florin you'll meet Buttercup, a princess longing to be united with her prince charming, Westley, as well as fractured characters fraught with problems: an impressive lisping clergyman; a spoiled and smarmy son of a king; a vile count, who attempts to kill Westley; and a gentle giant named Fezzik—with really strong arms!

I enjoy this movie so much because it plays to the fractured quality of marriage and life. After all, in real life "once upon a time" soon enough reads *Once Upon a Potty,* and like Westley, Rick and I also have been held captive in the Pit of Despair.

You see, the problem with most fairy tales is this: They only tell you one, rose-colored side of the story. They *don't* tell you the rest of the story.

For instance, I'm willing to bet Cinderella's once-dainty feet swelled up like puffer fish during pregnancy! And I would also hazard a guess that those delicate glass slippers probably shattered into a thousand pieces when she attempted to stuff her feet into them during a postpartum tizzy!

And really, don't you think that somewhere down the matrimonial road Snow White *had* to question what kind of prince goes around kissing seemingly dead girls? Well, it's time to wake up, throw back an espresso or two, and get out of fairy-tale living and into real life!

Love Changes

What trips up many couples is the wrong-headed belief that *passion* will be the active ingredient in a lasting relationship and that *maintaining romantic love* is the key to marital happiness.

"Fact is, love changes," says Les Parrott III, co-author of *Saving Your Marriage Before It Starts*. "There is an ebb and flow to it. When romance is present, life is wonderful. But we cannot demand this of love or of our partner."[5]

Too often couples stumble into this startling discovery long after the "I do's" have been exchanged, the rented tuxedos returned, and the mortgages cosigned. Resulting—for couples who commit to marriage under this pretense—in the predictable: Their unions flounder.

Statistics tell us that in America today more than half of first marriages end in divorce. Perhaps many of those marital failings could be traced back to the two needy strangers who unquestioningly believed the pop-culture fairy tale that love will indeed conquer all. The best thing we can do as husbands and wives is to recognize the *stages* every marriage goes through—regardless of romance, passion, or financial difficulty. And then, instead of viewing the appearance of each stage as a blow to our happily-ever-after worldviews, we can learn from them and reach the heavenly beginning, middle, and ending that God desires for us as man and wife.

Five Stages of Marriage

Darryl E. Owens, in an online article at www.familydigest.com, expounds on these stages in a concise and articulate manner. As I read through his words I was struck again by the stages Rick and I have already weathered during our 15 years of marriage. It is so good to know—so encouraging to be able to look back on what has happened and know—that you've actually made some headway in this thing called marriage. I think you'll identify quite readily the stage in which you're living now.

Stage 1: Romance

Couples inaugurate marriage in a state of romantic bliss. In this euphoric phase—which usually lasts from the first to the third years of marriage—newlyweds wear the proverbial rose-colored glasses. Life is perfect. Love is perfect. Their spouse is perfect. Marriage is viewed in an idealized manner. Differences are discounted, faults are few. Each thinks the other's idiosyncrasies are cute and sweet rather than irritating.

Stage 2: Faultfinding

The second stage is disappointment time. The way your spouse has of leaving the cap off the toothpaste that once was so cute now sticks in your craw. Partners realize that their spouse's behavior is irritating or even hurtful.

This stage is fraught with danger, and it's when many marriages end in divorce. These couples do not know how to effectively communicate their negative feelings to each other, nor do they know how to argue and problem-solve; and they are ignorant about negotiation and compromise. They never get beyond the faultfinding and blaming.

The intensity and turmoil of this stage varies among couples, but almost every couple engages in the struggle. It does not have to torpedo the marriage. Successful passage through this stage enables each partner to say, "Okay, so I am willing to admit that my romance with a perfect partner is an illusion. However, I am still fascinated with the mystery of who you are, and I am willing to pursue romance with you and journey together toward a more mature love."

Many couples stay mired in stage two. Stung by the hurt and damage inflicted during those tumultuous times, many couples divorce.

Stage 3: Cooperation

Stage three is as a breath of fresh air for couples who have stayed the course and successfully navigated the perilous passage of power struggles. Now a sense of acceptance and a willingness to change enters the relationship.

Stage 4: Acceptance

Stage four—acceptance, commitment, and mutuality—is where you and your mate realize that regardless of who you're with, there will be problems, so you might as well stay in the relationship and work them out. The challenge every couple faces is not to realize their expectations—but to realign their attitude and adjust to and accept the reality that the person they married will not and cannot meet all their needs all the time.

Togetherness just feels secure, and there exists a heightened sense of belonging. The unhealthy patterns that dogged their relationship seem ancient history. This acceptance is the bridge to ultimate transformation and a love that can be enjoyed for a lifetime.

Stage 5: Transformation

Stage-five couples develop "a web of meaningful interrelationships that support the marriage and deepen the joy." Couples who put in the time and effort reap this final reward. Intimacy is second nature. The attitude is "we grow together." They can reflect on the ups and downs, the bumps and bruised egos along the journey, and look forward to good times ahead. In this final stage, couples know what the fairy tales neglected to mention: *Love is hard work.*[6]

Beyond Fairy Tales

I think Rick and I have meandered through each of the stages mentioned above. And we've stayed in some of them for longer than we care to admit. We have found—much as you and your spouse have learned perhaps—that "this thing called love" is incredibly complex and infinitely changing from year to year in our life together.

And we've drawn one sure conclusion between us:

Love is indeed hard work.

And just like any work that is difficult, it brings its own sweet rewards at the end of a long hard day—or year! Love isn't attaining some ethereal state of "happily ever after." It is about going through the good and the bad, the joyous and the mundane, *together*. Love is about remaining *there*—during the worst of times, the best of times, and—most importantly—all the times.

Truth be told, sometimes the prince turns out to be a toad, and the princess, a real pain in the tiara. And oftentimes the dragons aren't slain and the good guy doesn't prevail—in fact, sometimes the bad guy wins.

But that's okay. In fact it's more than okay, for the vows that you and I uttered go far beyond the shallow expectations of a children's fairy tale. Our vows travel as deep as death…until it alone parts us.

Debtly Sin #3
Crafty Communications

6

Don't Ask, Don't Tell

Over the course of our marriage, Rick and I have implemented the oft-quoted military phrase of the 1990s when dealing with (okay, *avoiding*) our financial status as a couple.

Rick wouldn't ask and I didn't tell.

Living as a single-income family on his middle-management salary, we've known the reality of living from paycheck to paycheck and making partial bill payments in order to have enough cash on hand for crazy expenditures like milk and groceries. I remember one time in particular when Juicy Juice, Cheerios, and scrambled eggs were the dinner of choice four out of seven nights a week. We have lived in a land of financial clichés for more years than I care to think about.

Robbing Peter to pay Paul.

Spinning all our plates.

Counting our chickens before they hatched.

Putting all our eggs in one basket.

What a mess! And what pressure all that robbing, spinning, counting, and putting placed on our marriage.

Perhaps this is a good time to expand upon the money personalities that Rick and I possess. Truly, the temperament qualities (per chapter 1) that he and I both possess and express have played a tremendous role in our committing the debtly sin of crafty communications.

Just the Facts

I consider myself to be an optimist, and I generally see the sunny side of life.

The glass of life is half-full and just waiting to be filled to overflowing. Nothing is impossible—in fact, I often beg God for the impossible!

Rick will tell you I have a strong bent toward "reality avoidance." I can—and often do—live in a la-la-land of magical bank deposits and expect (there's that unrealistic expectation thing popping up again) manna-like checks to descend from heaven. I *really believe* those things are going to happen.

Okay, I'm insane.

You also need to know one other thing—I do not like being the bearer of bad news. *Ever.* So, regarding any and all negative checkbook balances, outstanding debts, and promised but unfulfilled repayments—I remained mute. Believe it or not, this strong **I**-personality (see page 27)—this "must-talk" woman—somehow managed to keep quiet about all things pertaining to money.

Now, Rick tends to paint his worldview with brushstrokes of gray.

His glass of life is half-empty and probably full of spoiled milk or flat soda.

But do not fear—he'll never succumb to botulism or anything like that. If a drink or food item has been left out longer than, say, 13 minutes, he will tentatively sniff it, hand it to one of our innocent children, and request, "Here, check this for Daddy."

I like to describe the love of my life as being "pessimistically realistic."

What that means is this: If he hears a faint odd noise coming from the van's motor (so faint in fact that he has to pull over to the shoulder, turn off the radio, and grumble, "Sshh, ssh. Listen—did you hear that?"), in his world it's automatically a cracked head or some belt that can be replaced only at the expense of the entire engine being removed, the wheels taken off, and the carpeting replaced!

Pessimistically realistic.

So, regarding bad news or the discussion of financial facts that make one run for the Pepsid AC, Rick didn't want to hear anything any more than I wanted to tell it.

So he didn't ask. He simply ignored such distasteful things and hoped they would all eventually go away. (Which was the same way he dealt with a poopy-diapered child wandering aimlessly around him years ago—amazing!)

And the Walls Came A-Tumblin' Down

We were able to ignore things until 1997. That's when our built-on-sand foundation crumbled.

In near-biblical proportions, the shouts of creditors, medical payments, and a new pay scale because of a career change of Rick's toppled our Jericho-sized walls of denial and debtly sin. Depression set in.

I would sleep during the daytime hours, hoping to escape for just a few blissful hours the haranguing phone calls of creditors and the sinking sensation of financial failure.

I found myself withholding emotionally more and more of myself from Rick, and the intimacy that we had once reveled in as man and wife became cold and perfunctory. Little by little I sensed my heart hardening against him, yet I no longer had the energy or the inclination to do anything about it.

One evening, in a fit of frustration, Rick sat down and attempted to make sense of our monthly expenses and income. He lasted about three hours. At one point, he threw his hands up in the air and muttered just loud enough for me to hear, "What am I working for anyway—she's spending every dime I make."

Needless to say, that didn't go over too well.

But again, instead of facing our problems and discussing them in as calm and reasonable a manner as possible, we simply didn't ask and didn't tell. We withdrew from one another and from the cold hard realities of where our debtly living had brought us.

There we were, in our early 30s with no savings other than the children's birthday cash that we confiscated on occasion, a spotty record of giving to our church, and a credit rating that could virtually guarantee our never enjoying an interest rate of 28 percent or less.

Reaping What We Didn't Sow

Maybe you're wondering what a "don't ask, don't tell" moment looks or sounds like in a marriage. Let me share a specific incident from our tawdry financial past, as well as the lesson we learned from it—years down the road.

I have always kept the checkbook and paid the bills in our marriage.

And while I'm no mathematical genius I was always able to do a pretty good job—balancing the account each month and paying bills in a timely and responsible manner. That is, until around 1992. I still don't know what it was completely, but after a particularly difficult transfer from a community we loved to a city we despised, I steadily became less and less competent in my role as a money manager.

Where we had once faithfully given to our church, we now found ourselves sitting at home on Sunday mornings and pocketing the designated tithe by default.

This was a major "don't tell" matter with Rick and me. We had both experienced the faithfulness of God's provision in our past and had given without hesitation during the first six years of our marriage.

But here in this new city—where I had attended an adult Sunday school class and broken down in tears of loneliness, only to be ignored and never even touched by any of the women around me—I found myself hardening up.

I willfully chose to quit trying.

I willfully chose to withhold our giving.

And I willfully chose to not tell Rick about it.

This continued for several years—even after we moved yet again and found community within another church setting. It continued despite financial windfalls and increases in Rick's base salary. And all we seemed to accomplish was digging a deeper and deeper pit of money problems and worries.

Then one afternoon we were having dinner with some family members, and a comment was made about the importance of the tithe in Christian living. "Well, we tithe," Rick commented, "but we seem to be worse off than ever before!"

Now, here's the point I want to make. The issue at hand wasn't whether God does or does not bless one financially because one gives a certain percentage of one's earnings to the church.

The issue was this: Rick believed I was tithing.

I was not.

Nor had I done so for some time, as I told you before.

But somehow, somewhere along the lines of marital communication, we had mastered the art of "don't ask, don't tell" and managed to withhold every truth—even biblical, good-Christians-should-know-better truth—from one another.

I didn't speak up in that moment.

I didn't want to incur Rick's anger nor hear the speech concerning giving that I was sure would come if I did.

But later—try several years later—Rick confessed this to me: "Julie, I knew you weren't mailing the tithe checks back to our previous church when we lived in Iowa. And I noticed that you seldom placed an envelope in the offering plate in Illinois. I knew. But I didn't want to ask you about it." He went on to admit, "I just didn't want to deal with it—so I kept silent and just figured the issue would come up sooner or later."*

Needless to say, the issue of "don't ask, don't tell" did eventually surface, and it was joined at the hip with yet another form of crafty communication!

---

* Whew—that's an honest confession if I ever heard one! Let's give Rick a hand for coming clean because it's sure not easy telling your mistakes to the world—or even just to wonderful readers like you!

7

The Art of
Compassionate Censorship

I don't want to admit this, but here goes—I am a liar.

Wait, wait—please don't take this book back and demand a refund from your innocent bookstore manager, and please don't write angry letters to the publisher! For despite the ugliness of that confession, I believe that lying is a debtly sin at work in far more lives and marriages than we care to admit. There are in fact, countless men or women who find themselves uttering Slinky-like fabrications about money and responsibilities—all of which enable them to maneuver their way about and around their speaking absolute truth regarding their finances and how those finances will affect their spouse.

Now, I never actually referred to my debtly sin as "lying." Covering it with a friendly financial-loser veneer, I often referred to this "weakness" as the *art of compassionate censorship*.

In the past, *compassionate censorship* led to my applying for a credit card in my own name. It was necessary, I *compassionately* told myself, if we were to meet the ever-increasing "end of the month" shortages that we so often faced.

However (shades of censorship creeping in now), I knew Rick would never approve. So I rationalized the deed by telling myself that he just didn't have to know how bad things were. In fact, I was probably doing him a favor by taking care of this all by myself and not worrying him! (Oh boy!)

Compassionate censorship also led me to believe that I could actually have a credit card and "use it only in case of emergency." Just so you know—me being truthful and all—"in case of emergency" for this financial loser often entailed a meal charged at Red Lobster and a trip to the movie theatre, courtesy of Visa.

"In case of emergency" is the Grand Poo-Bah of all credit-card lies.

Emergency! Emergency!

My "in case of" came January 10 of that same year. It was then I gave birth to our third child—Patrick Michael—a nine-pound-eleven-ounce bundle of future medical costs.

At the age of eight weeks he suffered an acute croup attack. His tiny airway made it nearly impossible for him to breathe, and Rick and I had to stand by helplessly as three paramedics knelt on our living-room floor and administered oxygen to our tiny son. Patrick was hospitalized for several days, and less than two weeks after his returning home he was diagnosed with severe sleep apnea. Within a few weeks time we had incurred medical expenses that were not covered by our insurance but were absolute emergencies. I paid for them with my Visa and maintained my *compassionate* composure (that is, I never shared this information with Rick).

Although he looked robust and healthy, Patrick continued to battle pneumonia, bronchitis, and other upper-respiratory illnesses throughout his first 18 months of life. The overnight stays in pediatric hospital wings, as well as three-hour drives to asthma specialists in Iowa City, Iowa, necessitated extra meals and gasoline costs.

All of which fell under the category of "in case of emergency" needs.

Eight months after covertly obtaining said credit card, I found myself drowning in $2200 of "in case of emergency" debt—on which I could no longer eke out the minimum payment (a minimum payment that Rick knew nothing about).

The metaphorical plates had all been spun, and each one was shattering about my feet. I had robbed Peter to pay Paul so often that they banded together, formed a savings and loan, and denied me credit! And the chicken, after seeing all her eggs breaking in one basket, attempted to hang herself from the fraying noose.

I was out of clever metaphors and euphemisms. Compassionate censorship had all but ruined me. I had *lied* to my husband, and my sin was about to be found out. (As with countless other moments in my life and marriage, I recorded it in my journal.)

Date: 11/13/96
> I just told Rick about the $2200 I owe on the credit card. "Why didn't you tell me we were in such bad shape?" he repeated time and time again.

I answered back, "If you really wanted to know you could have asked me at any time—where did you think the money was coming from to buy the gas to Iowa and for the noncovered medical bills?"

He threatened to take the checkbook and "just do it myself!"

But he won't.

He'll just get frustrated and tell me how he can't possibly figure out the mess I've made.

I know it will all come back to me.

He's angry. Quietly angry.

I wish he would yell. At least I'd know he was feeling something—anger, disappointment—anything. But he doesn't speak. And neither do I.

And the scary thing is this. I don't really care anymore.

Not as much as I did six months ago when we had a similar blowup.

Or the time before that.

We just go on about our business, attempting to shore up what is horribly broken—our finances and the "us" of being a couple.

And I wonder—how much longer until "we" can no longer be fixed, or one of us simply quits?

Liar, Liar, Pants on Fire!

Liar: a person who tells lies. *To lie:* to make a statement or statements that one knows to be false, especially with intent to deceive. *To deceive:* to make a person believe what is not true.

In the August 2001 issue of *Reader's Digest* magazine, writer Louise Lague incorporated the results of a telephone poll involving 1000 married couples in her article titled "How Honest Are Couples, Really?" Each spouse was asked specific questions regarding truthfulness and marriage.

Can you guess which marital issue was most frequently lied about between husbands and wives?

If you answered money, moola, greenbacks, or any derivative thereof, you got it! Forty-eight percent (nearly half!) of both husbands and wives said they had "hushed up" the truth concerning how much they had paid for something they had bought.

In other words, they lied. One wife of 43 years made the following comment: "I don't like to tell him how much I spend when I go shopping. I'm afraid he'll cut back on the budget."[7] That's nearly 500 individuals who fessed up to the debtly sin of compassionate censorship—nearly 500 people who in essence said, "I am a liar."

You see, I'm not the only one who's committed this debtly sin. But believe me, I'm not throwing a party. And I know you're not either! Because those of us who have struggled or who are struggling with compassionate censorship know the true cost it exacts from our marriages and our own desire for integrity. We may give a knowing smirk as a friend shows us her "secret stash" of purchases hidden in the back of her closet. A husband may tell himself that it's none of his wife's concern when purchasing a home-theater sound system against her earlier express wishes. And many of us may try to convince ourselves that compassionate censorship is a neglible matter in the grand scheme of life.

But I boldly disagree. For compassionate censorship—lying—no matter how it is displayed or communicated, is in fact sin. And sin, as a Southern gospel song declared, will always take you further than you want to go, keep you longer than you want to stay, and cost you more than you want to pay.

In all likelihood you're feeling pretty lousy about this.

And that's not such a bad thing. After all, it isn't until an alcoholic acknowledges his drunkenness that he can truly begin to find help. And a gambler has to face his addictive behavior, as well as its uncontrolled nature, before relief can be found. All sinners—all sins—have to be confessed and faced up to before forgiveness and healing can occur. And so it is with lying.

Woe Is Me!

One of my favorite chapters in the Bible is found in the book of Romans, chapter 7, beginning at verse 14.

The apostle Paul—who before his encounter with Jesus the Christ, relished persecuting and killing Jesus' followers—poignantly expresses the battle that a Christian fights: light against darkness, right against wrong, good against evil.

He writes in verse 15 of chapter 7, "That which I am doing, I do not understand; for I am not practicing what I would like to do, but I am doing the very thing I hate!" He agonizes again in verses 19 and 20, "The good that I wish, I do not do; but I practice the very evil that I do not wish. But if I am doing the very thing I do not wish, I am no longer the one doing it, but sin which dwells in me."

Whew! I don't know about you, but I am both relieved and cut to the quick as I read these words. Relieved by the knowledge that Paul himself battled against sin's pull, cut to the quick that it is indeed sin that lives within me.

Here's truth you can bank on: Lying is sin that will destroy your relationship with God and with your spouse. Sin that will take you further—in this case, often into debt—than you ever imagined. Sin that will keep you longer—in my case, close to eight years of active lying in marriage—than you want to stay. And sin that will cost you more than you ever wanted to pay.

Your marriage.

Debtly Sin #4

Trivial Pursuits

8

I Possess, Therefore I Am

There's a hymn that I remember singing as a young girl, and one of the verses went something like this: "My hope is built on nothing less than Jesus' blood and righteousness; I dare not trust the sweetest frame, but wholly lean on Jesus' name."[8]

I haven't sung that old hymn for some time now. And if I did, I would have to admit sadly that my financial-loser lyrics would sound something like this: "My hope is built on nothing less than ATMs and get-rich schemes. I dare not live within my means, but charge my cards to the extreme."

Let me get the proverbial cards out on the table. It won't require sleight of hand nor will it take up much writing space because I'm not playing with a full deck. (Proceed only when you have wiped that smirk off your face!) I have but one card to lay down, but it's a dandy! It's the trump card to trump all trumps! And it often compels me to participate in a royal flush of manic activity at my local Target store. So here it is in all its profound and shallow glory:

I like money, and I like the things that money buys. A lot.

- Earrings marked 75 percent off the already discounted price? Like 'em.

- Gourmet chocolate chunk ice cream cone available at O'Hare International Airport in Chicago? Like it.

- *Southern Living, Life, InStyle,* and *Allure* magazines? Like those too.

- Christian Book Distributors package deals? Really, really like 'em!

Not only do I like the things that money buys…I am fatally drawn to all things thought to be the finer things of life.

On Being a Bon Vivant

The French understand people like this.

They're referred to as bon vivants, and just pronouncing it makes you feel oh-so-European. Go ahead, try it: bahn vee-VANT. Honestly, don't you have a craving for a crêpe or something? Webster's dictionary defines a bon vivant as "a person with refined taste, especially one who enjoys superb food and drink." Well, here's the Julie Barnhill definition: a person with an innate attraction to things they can't afford and food they should not eat.

In a blindfold test a true bon vivant will recognize brand over generic in a Donna-Karan-New-York minute! We appreciate the discrepancy in serving portions at the

Chateau Rouge versus the Sirloin Stockade, as well as the price differential.

It's simply a bon-vivant thing.

I Like It, I Like It a Lot!

Now the issue with living as a bon vivant is this: There will always be more *stuff* than you can shake a refined walking stick at—and it will always be calling your name!

Sometime in the early 1980s, my best friend and I confiscated an R-rated comedy album from her brother's LP collection and slithered off to listen to its adult content behind her closed (and locked!) bedroom door.

We laughed so hard our sides hurt! Granted, we also familiarized ourselves with a few phrases that up until that moment we'd never heard. While much of the material was tasteless—funny, but tasteless—I have never forgotten the comedian's diatribe on "stuff."

"All you need in life is a little place for your stuff," he said—and then went on to explain that the "little place" was, indeed, your house. He accurately observed that a house oftentimes is simply a pile of stuff with a cover on it!

Hmm...he has a point. As I type these words I'm looking around my "little place" and noting all the furniture, bookshelves, wall hangings, oak flooring, crown molding, window treatments, and kitchen gadgets that overflow it. And once I gaze outside the windows of my "little place" I note the patches of crabgrass and dandelion weeds that thwart Rick's valiant treatments of yard "stuff." I also nod to the irritating pea gravel that is soon to be replaced with a carpet of smooth, black, asphalt "stuff." Indeed, the Barnhills' house is a pile of stuff—inside and out—with a cover! (And that cover, by the way, was completely replaced less than six years ago.)

Now, hear me out. I'm not recommending that you embrace Mr. George Carlin as your financial or spiritual guru! But—his observations nail the skewed love affair that many of us financial losers have with accumulating, getting, possessing, hoarding, owning, and simply having *stuff*.

Let's face it. There isn't much stuff in or on God's green earth that I and other financial losers don't want! And the more stuff we have? Well, it seems like we only want more.

It's a Stuff-Mart World

So what's wrong with that? you may be asking. Maybe you think I'm going to hit you with a call to sell all you have and go live in the plains of Montana. Relax. I'm not about to say that! Nor am I trying to put some guilt trip on you for having a list of "things to get" at your local Target store.

Nope. That's not what this is about.

But here's what it is about. The problem with getting caught up in the acquiring-and-possessing syndrome of our culture, the problem with living to get and getting to live, the problem with having a house (as well as a minivan) full of stuff is this: All those things rarely satisfy. The red Kitchen Aid mixer that you've longed for since 1987 will quickly lose its luster. And soon enough you'll be looking for "one more thing" to complete your kitchen. The "4-bedroom, 4-bath, whirlpool in the master bath" home that you just sank all your equity into will, at some point, lose its luster too.

And the more enamored we become with the shiny new things around us, the more space, energy, time, and money it takes to keep up with keeping up!

Stuff and Mayhem

Ilyce Glink, a financial planner and author of the book *50 Simple Things You Can Do to Improve Your Personal Finances,* has this comment:

> When you buy a bigger home to accommodate your stuff, you pay higher taxes, higher heating bills, bigger cooling bills, a bigger mortgage, plus whatever the upkeep costs are for the stuff itself![9]

Maintaining and expanding the stuff you already have takes a lot of money and time. And I'm not just talking houses. Simple things like a Nintendo mushroom into Xboxes and PlayStations. Or consider "stuff" like family vacations. Just going to a regional theme park will set you back several hundred dollars nowadays. And Disneyland? Well, you might have to win an Olympic gold medal before you could actually vacation there! But don't forget sporting events like professional baseball games. Whoo-eee! Rick and I took in a game in Atlanta a year ago, and we ended up splitting a meal between us. Take it from a bon vivant—no hot dog is worth $13! Or you can sign your son up for the junior football league and be prepared to put down a deposit just shy of your monthly mortgage payment.

Now, I realize many of you reading this earn considerably more dollars than Rick and I. Others of you are keeping a family together on minimum-wage incomes alone. It isn't my intention to make this a class-versus-class debate. Rather, I want to bring to the forefront of our financial-loser attention this simple fact: Many of us are swimming in debt and marital mayhem as the result of nothing more than a whacked-out need for possessing and accumulating stuff. The truth is, much of the financial mayhem in our marriages could be brought to an end if we would simply stop accumulating and start being satisfied with the things we already have.

9

You Look Marvelous!

Comedian Billy Crystal is famous for his dead-on impersonation of the late Fernando Lamas, a courtly gentleman if there ever was one.

Crystal's trademark line—"You look marvelous!"—was inspired by a real-life encounter. According to Crystal, he ran into Lamas on a day that he, Crystal, was not feeling so well. Lamas quickly boosted his spirits with the following observation: "Well, Billy, you *look* marvelous. And you know, it is better to look marvelous than to feel marvelous!"*

Ah, Fernando, how well I relate to your way of thinking! If there is a debtly sin that I've committed (and I'm listing seven), this preoccupation with appearance and all the outward stuff that money can buy would be number one. In our 15 years of marriage, I would have to say that, by and large, most of our financial low points have come as a result

_____

* For those readers old enough to know what I'm talking about, put your lips together, scrunch your eyebrows, and say it with me: "You look maaaah-ve-luss!"

of my desire to look marvelous, or at the very least, to have an appearance of marvelous!

I've wanted my hair, clothes, house, yard—yikes!—even my bathroom baseboards to have that put-together, I've-got-it-going-now look. I guess you could say I've gotten a tad obsessive.

A quick illustration will prove I'm right.

Appearance—On Credit

In 1992, I was shopping with three of the most fabulous girlfriends that a woman could have. Each of them—Becky, Lisa, and Diana—had laughed so hard at something I had said that they'd snorted, and I always had such a great time with them.

I loved being with these women, and there weren't too many weekends during the years 1990 to 1993 that we weren't either hanging out with our husbands at Bill and Becky's house or participating in an all-girl, manic, shop-till-you-drop spree in and around St. Louis, Missouri.

On this particular day I had spent very little money.

Truth be told (which it wasn't, since I was right in the midst of the compassionate censorship phase of my life), I didn't have an honest dime to my name, but I wasn't about to share that with my girlfriends! So I kept up the appearance of browsing and became the token "bag carrier" for the others as they tried on clothes, and so on.

Then at last I actually purchased something. It was a double-doozie-creme-filled chocolate-chip cookie—actually, it must have been *several* double-doozies because I used my credit card to pay for the purchase.

Yes, you read that correctly. I used a credit card to make a cookie transaction. Is that sad or what?

Then Becky walked up beside me and decided to purchase something too. She also pulled a credit card from her billfold and handed it to the clerk. And that's when it caught my eye.

It being Becky's credit card.

It was shiny and new. *Mine* was all smudgy and beat-up.

It had a cool holographic eagle-thing on it. *Mine* had none.

It was made of gold! All right, plastic, but gold-hued plastic!

I looked down at my smudgy, beat-up, non-holographic-security-symbol credit card and observed its color. It was brown. Brown as in plain, boring, paper-bag brown. Drop-it-on-the-ground-on-a-rainy-day-and-lose-it brown. With nary a glimmer of gold or a holographic reflection in sight I realized that my credit card looked really ugly. So there I stood, fretting over my dull, boring Visa card and wishing I had a pretty gold one like my pal Becky.

But here's the really sad part. The balance on that dull brown credit card was over $3200, with a minimum monthly payment of around $40. Rick's monthly take-home pay in those early years of our marriage was just a little more than $1000—and here's a look at our monthly "budget" at the time:

Rent	$375	Water bill	$20
Electricity	$75	Diapers, formula, baby stuff	$60
Gas bill	$45		
Phone bill	$80	Oh, yes, food for Rick and me	$150
Student loan	$62		
Car payments	$300	Gas for automobiles	$75

Now, you don't have to be Larry Burkett or Mary Hunt to see what this math was adding up to!

By 1992, I had been treading water in the pool of marital debt and minimum payments for five years. But it would be five more before the walls of Jericho fell and I owned up to the grip of appearance on my thinking and spending.

Roots of Deceit

It's imperative that we, as financial losers, understand the root cause of this debtly sin of deceptive appearances.

It isn't enough that I deem it a debtly sin. Our definition must come from an irrefutable source of truth and wisdom. (No—Cleo the Jamaican psychic doesn't fit the bill either. Besides, she's being sued in federal court for fraud anyway!) In this case we need to turn to the one financial manual that has stood the test of time, the Holy Bible. After all, this sin of deceit that wreaks havoc in our lives and marriages has actually been around for some time—try since the beginning of time.

Eve had it all.

Perfectly and lovingly shaped by the Creator, she was the perfect complement to her divinely formed counterpart, Adam. Forget the gospel according to Hooters, *Sports Illustrated,* or *All My Children!* Eve was the quintessential XX-chromosome package.

And Eve lived in paradise. Literally. She didn't have to load up a minivan and shove a fistful of coupons in her purse to shop. She simply walked around, chose from the abundant display that God Himself provided, and spent quality time with Him and Adam.

Everything Eve needed was provided in the garden.

She had it all, including that perfect male specimen named Adam.

Eve's life was, by all appearances, perfect.

Then one day, starting at verse 1 of chapter 3 in the book of Genesis, all perfect appearances changed. You may know the story well. Eve, we are told, engaged in a conversation with a crafty creature called "the serpent." (Interesting to note that his mode of communication was deceit and lies!) And somehow through that craftiness he was able to deceive Eve and convince her that it was indeed okay to eat of a fruit tree that God Himself had instructed her and Adam to avoid. And here's what I find most interesting (looking at chapter 3, verse 6): "When the woman saw that the tree was good for food, and that it was a delight to the eyes, and that the tree was desirable to make one wise...she ate." The New International Version translates the phrase describing the tree as "pleasing to the eye."

Very interesting. Perhaps Eve had imagined something plain and of everyday appearance. But surely not the delectable and appealing fruit she pulled from the tree's branch.

I have to tell you, I am shaken by the debtly reality foreshadowed in chapter 3 of Genesis. Eve's attraction simply to the outward *appearance* of that fruit flourished into an action that, after Adam's evil choice, changed all human history. So, I am shaken—because far too many times I have been deceived by the *appearance* of things—things that then tie up my time, hem in my actions, and ultimately take my attention far, far away from what is eternally important and financially prudent. Make no mistake, dear fellow financial loser—the same enemy who wooed Eve is still at work, lulling each of us into spending and debtly mistakes. In his craftiness he needs no new tricks up his sleeves either. He continues to entice us into debtly sin through the simple appearance of the things that appeal to our eyes.

Debtly Sin #5
Discontent

10

Fun House Mirrors

As the drawn-out summer days of August come to an end, our local community celebrates the beginning of a new school year and the promise of fall.

Rotary Club members set up a tent and sell grilled pork-chop and steak sandwiches, 4-H members volunteer their time and mix up some delicious Lemonade Shakeups, while Boden Amusement provides the mandatory thrill rides, such as the upside-down Salt-and-Pepper Shaker and the Scrambler.

Armband night (when you can ride endlessly for a mere $8 a wristband) finds Rick, Kristen, Ricky Neal, Patrick, and me walking a gauntlet of corn dog vendors and food stands set up to sell funnel cakes, elephant ears, and cotton candy. It's the one time the children can see their dad race down a gigantic 23-foot high super-slide on a postage-stamp-sized gunny sack and can each attempt to break last fall's record of consecutive rides on the Tilt-a-Whirl. And each year the children beg Rick or me to accompany them through the carnival's Fun House.

Fun House, Schmun House

I have issues with fun houses.

And they can all be traced back to 1972 and the Missouri State Fair in Sedalia, Missouri. I was seven years old at that time and was having a wonderful time with my dad at this annual summer event. We had previewed all the blue-ribbon 4-H* projects and had taken a quick look at the bearded lady. Who I now realize simply had a problem with pesky chin hairs!

We drank gallons of soda, watched tractors pull over-sized loads of concrete blocks, and sweat like crazy in the humid summer heat. That's how we happened upon the air-conditioned Fun House.

Dad walked ahead of me, and I remember giggling as the floor moved beneath our feet. A few more steps ahead and the floor slanted, making it nearly impossible to walk forward. *Hey! This is fun*, I thought, and I continued to make my way through a darkened hallway.

Then we came to a fork in the road. You could turn left and make your way out of the building or turn right and continue on with the frivolity. The only problem was, if you wanted to go right, you would have to walk through… drum roll, please…the revolving Fun Barrel.

This of course is a great big hollow cylinder that rotates again and again and again, never slowing, never stopping. As a seven-year-old I was most concerned about the "never stopping." Of course, my dad had no idea I was experiencing my first anxiety attack, so he promptly veered right and walked through the spinning barrel—never stopping and never faltering. He assumed that his seven-year-old daughter was right behind him.

He assumed wrong.

---

* 4-H is the youth education branch of the Cooperative Extension Service, a program of the United States Department of Agriculture. Each H identifies an area of growth potential: head, heart, hands, and health.

While dear old Dad faded into the distance I broke out into a cold sweat. Just contemplating having to walk through the turning cylinder had me sweating bullets of fear! But what choice did I have? My dad had left—who knew where he was at the time? I had no choice. It was now or never. Finally, I took a deep breath and took a step into what I was sure would become my revolving circle of death.

And that's exactly how far I got...one step. All my resolve melted into a puddle of defeat as I fell flat on my backside and watched the red-and-white candy stripes inside the barrel spin on and on.

Three hours later (okay, it was probably closer to 30 seconds, but does it really matter when you're rolling around like a disabled hamster?) my dad realized I wasn't behind him. Or it may have been the wails echoing off the walls throughout the Fun House that tipped him off. Suffice it to say, after being rescued from the depths of that barrel I vowed never to set foot (or bottom) in one again.

Been There, Done That

Which of course leads me 20-plus years down the road, to a point where I'm listening to Kristen and Ricky beg me to walk through the Fall Festival Fun House with them.

Well, after that long a time I figured it was time to face my fear, so I took a deep breath, swallowed a shot of my Lemonade Shakeup, and headed for the entrance. Their father guarded the exit, trying to reassure 18-month-old Patrick that he would see Mommy again.

I'm proud to say that I made it safely through the barrel, as did the two children. We continued on until we discovered the Fun House Wall of Mirrors. Oh my! What a room. Everywhere you looked you could see a hilarious reflection of yourself. To my right, I stood two feet tall and bore an uncanny resemblance to Patrick. Looking straight ahead, I could count at least 32 images of Kristen but was unable to discern which one was actually her. I continued walking, hoping to make my way out of the labyrinth, when suddenly—I saw it...or better said, I saw her.

Her being *me*.

But not just plain-ol'-everyday-Julie-Ann-Barnhill me—but rather, an absolute stunning me—standing five feet, eleven inches, and weighing in at around 125 pounds. I just couldn't quit staring and marveling at the reflection before me.

My stomach was positively concave! My legs seemed to go on forever, and my face—well, my face was slim, my jawline taut, and as far as I was concerned, I looked like a perfect 10.

I loved this room! Better said, I loved the mirror, and I continued to stand there and stare.

My reverie was broken a few minutes...hours...days later when the faint sound of Rick's pleading and Patrick's loud crying interrupted my dreaming. "Julie," Rick begged, "the kids and I miss you—please come on out...the baby's messy."

But I didn't want to leave.

For the first time in my life I actually saw myself tall and skinny. No woman in her right mind would walk away from that! Granted, it wasn't really me I was seeing, but it sure beat the five feet-four-inch, not-125-pound woman that greeted me each morning in the bathroom mirror at 17 Lakelawn Drive!

Would You Like a Little Distortion with That?

It wasn't until several days later that I finally came to my senses.

If I recall correctly, it was a piece of chocolate mousse that beckoned me back to the land of the short and pudgy. But I've never forgotten those few minutes alone with my thinner self and the incredible power that those distorted images had on my thinking and perception of myself.

We're all living in a world of fun-house mirrors.

There's a familiar Bible verse found in 1 Corinthians, chapter 13, verse 12. In it the apostle Paul speaks of one who is looking in a mirror and seeing, at best, a very dim and poor reflection of who one really is. (At the time Paul wrote those verses, mirrors from Corinth were considered to be the best of the best.)

It's vital to note that the Corinthian mirrors were not the clearly reflecting glass ones that are so common today. Rather, they were simply highly polished pieces of metal that reflected a distorted image of the one gazing into their sheen.

More than a few of us are staring intently into the world's version of fun-house mirrors. And more often than not, we allow those warped reflections to undermine the view we have of our spouse, our marriage, and even eternity.

The Mirrors of Comparison and Envy

Comparison and envy like to travel side by side. Much like in the Frank Sinatra classic "Love and Marriage," you can't have one without the other. I shared my own battle with the evil twins of comparison and envy in my first book, and it's worth confessing again.

Ten years ago I was invited to the home of a new acquaintance. I had met Stacey at church and thought that we might have a lot in common. She and her husband had eaten dinner at our home, and Stacey and I had agreed that we should get together for "mom" time at her place sometime the next week.

About three days later I called to get directions to her house and was taken aback at the street address she gave. She had named a certain subdivision out by the car dealership. But surely she hadn't meant *that* subdivision. It was in *the* neighborhood! You know what I'm talking about—every town has one. It's the neighborhood you tool through with your dissatisfied spouse on negative-checkbook weeks just to make yourself feel a little bit more lousy! It's the neighborhood that makes you curse your lot in life when you realize you couldn't even afford the lawn tractors being used to cut the lawns!

She lived there.

I packed up Ricky and Kristen and headed toward Stacey's.

To be honest—and I'm being painfully honest—I was hoping that she lived on a peripheral street of the neighborhood. I was hoping she lived in a house that bordered the neighborhood but didn't quite make the cut. I was hoping she lived in a neighborhood—well, like mine.

She didn't.

I pulled up into a concrete driveway—which made me nervous because our car leaked oil—and as she greeted the kids, my eyes were drawn to the gorgeous, professional landscape. That woman had more money in perennials than I had in my checking account! One bag of mulch equaled two cans of powdered baby formula in my neighborhood!

The children followed Stacey inside, and I slithered in behind. As I walked into her living room I heard myself gasp—out loud at that! There before my eyes was a room straight from an Ethan Allen showroom floor. The carpet was plush, the color of a white sand beach. Stylishly swagged across her windows were not cotton panels from the local K-Mart but exquisitely beautiful, cranberry-red draperies.

She led us through that stunning room, casually chatting with the children. I was beginning to feel sick to my stomach. With a faux smile plastered on my green face, I followed Stacey through her well-appointed home.

The refrigerator was the size of a small toolshed.

The snack bar chairs were upholstered in white leather.

And an enormous television screen filled the family-room wall.

Finally, we made our way down to the "play room"—or as it was referred to in my neighborhood, the basement—which looked a lot like my living room.

I believe it was at this point that I officially passed out!

You know what? I can't remember anything about that day other than the twisting knife of comparison and envy, which gutted my enjoyment. Stacey was a wonderful hostess; she made my children feel welcome, and I'm sure she was a pleasant conversationalist. However, I didn't hear a word she said. And that's because my covetous mind was evaluating and envying everything I saw in her home.

From the porcelain figurines in a cherry curio cabinet to the five-piece furniture suite in her ample master bedroom, I just couldn't stop comparing her things to mine. And the more I thought about it, the shorter my end of the stick seemed to be getting!

I never did see Stacey after that visit. And I think the reasons are pretty obvious. I allowed my warped and distorted thoughts to short-circuit any possibilities of a friendship.[10]

I have found envy to be one of the meanest, nastiest, and most vicious of sins.

Envy blurs my ability to see things distinctly and causes me to see the success of others as a threat. It also leads me to consider people—like Stacey—as the "competition," rather than as possible friends, those who might offer a relationship to be explored and enjoyed.

Envy is a very secret sin; it flourishes in the soil of denial and sends down roots of bitterness. It works as a corrosive agent in our spirits and marriage relationships and blinds us to the blessings, accomplishments, and rewards in our own life.

After years of struggle with comparison and envy, I am convinced that the desire to acquire is not so much out of a passion to possess (let alone the joy of possession) but rather comes out of a need to feel superior and "one-up" those who we feel inferior to. Trust me—this is a difficult subject for me to write about because I so often find myself right back "there" in that same place of wanting to outdo and out-achieve in an effort to prove that I am better or worthy of attention.

Like it or not, comparison and envy get to the heart of what debtly sinning is all about!

11

A Little Perspective, Please

The following is something to ponder.

If you woke up this morning in good health, you are more blessed than the million people who will not survive this week. If you have never experienced the danger of battle, the loneliness of imprisonment, the agony of torture, or the pangs of starvation, you are ahead of 500 million people in the world.

If you can attend a church meeting without fear of harassment, arrest, torture, or death—you are more blessed than three billion people in the world. If you have food in the refrigerator, clothes on your back, a roof overhead, and a place to sleep—you are richer than 75 percent of this world.

If you have money in the bank and in your wallet, and spare change in a dish someplace, you are among the top 8 percent of the world's wealthy. If you can read this, you are more blessed than more than two billion people in the world who cannot read at all.[11]

Did you catch the part about having food in your refrigerator, clothes on your back, a roof over you, and a place to sleep?

You are richer—yes, richer—than 75 percent of this world.

One Sunday our pastor asked the congregation to name aloud the wealthiest people in the world. Gates. Turner. The Donald—they all were mentioned. And then he read us the above paragraph. And while I grudgingly acknowledged that Rick and I had more than the vast majority of the world's population, I still thought we were far from being considered "rich." Several weeks later, the events of September 11, 2001, took place, and a dramatic shift in my thinking occurred.

You know where you were that Tuesday morning.

I had just sat down in front of my computer, hoping to meet a September 15 deadline for this manuscript. It had been my habit to click on www.drudgereport.com and get the latest news hit before writing, but I had recently recommitted myself to beginning the day with prayer and Scripture reading (that is, some *good* news) before dealing with the news of war, murder, and political intrigue.

A few moments after I had finished praying the phone rang. It was Rick, and I could tell by his voice that something was wrong.

"Julie, do you have the TV on?"

"No," I told him, "I just sat down to finish some chapters of the book—what's the matter?"

With our country's recent history of work-related violence I first thought that something had happened at the company where he worked. "Are *you* okay?" I asked.

His voice shook as he answered, "I'm all right but I need you to go online or turn on CNN and see what you can find out about a jet crashing into the World Trade Center in New York—we heard something on the radio about it, but we don't have any televisions here at the office and we don't know what's going on." He hesitated and then spoke again, "Call me back as soon as you know something—and Julie, I love you."

As I fumbled with the remote control, looking for a news channel, a sick "this is going to be bad" sensation overrode any hope of good news. It was the same sick feeling I had had while standing in front of a television screen in Muscatine, Iowa, watching the Texas compound of David Koresh burn to the ground. All the while listening to the television commentators informing viewers that women and small children were within its confines. It was the same feeling as I had had when I first heard of the terrorist bombing of the Murrah Building in Oklahoma City.

I turned on our television and watched—with untold millions across the world—the horrific replay of the second jet crashing into the south tower of the World Trade Center.

Gone

Now, writers are supposed to have all kinds of words to describe how they feel. In fact, I read a scathing editorial in a New York newspaper in which a journalist verbally beat up another for stating in his daily article that he "could not express the horror" of that day. But we all know that he wasn't the only one struggling to articulate the depth of his grief on that fall morning.

The only word (and a weak one at that) that could possibly sum up the state of my emotions from that cable news moment until nearly two weeks later is the word "blank."

As I knelt on our living-room floor and cried aloud in grief and fear for our nation, my soul felt *blank*.

As I watched thousands of terrified citizens try to outrun an enveloping cloud of debris, I felt *blank*.

And as I spoke with my friend Anne on that awful September morning, as I contemplated driving to school and picking up my children simply to touch them and to hold them—even then the down-deep feeling I was left with was one of blankness.

For nearly two weeks I walked around in a coma of nothingness. The manuscript that had been moving full steam ahead now sat untouched and unedited.

What's the point anyway? I asked Rick over and over again. *Am I supposed to write a book to help husbands and wives prepare for Armageddon?*

I couldn't do anything.

My 13-year-old daughter worried about the dark circles under my eyes. My husband and editors kept encouraging me to get back to work on the book. But I just couldn't. I had watched—with my own eyes—two buildings collapsing upon their steel supports, taking thousands of souls into eternity.

In a moment's time, men and women were gone. Never again to be held in the arms of those who loved them. Never to be heard from again. Never to be seen or caressed again.

Gone. And each of their loved ones would have nothing left of them save the wealth of memories of days and nights lived, a lifetime lived, before that time and that place.

An Incomprehensible Gift

Within an hour's time on September 11, the material things that vied for first place in our minds were relegated to "it just doesn't matter" status.

As I watched television anchors weeping with men and women who were desperately pleading for information about their loved ones, I was struck by how unimportant *things* were at that moment.

No one was risking their life to retrieve safety-deposit boxes.

No one was printing up leaflets in hopes of finding their automobile or rushing back into a hotel room to salvage their jewelry or designer clothes.

No, all anyone wanted in the initial hours and long days to come was to hear the voice of their beloved, or to feel the warmth of their hand nestled inside their own. All they wanted was to hold that irreplaceable someone again.

I'll never understand human nature.

Why does it seem that—until we've lost something that is truly worthy or have felt the terrifying threat of losing that something—we never appreciate what we have? I can see my husband, day in and day out, and get to a point where everything he says, or does, or even the way he walks, annoys me to no end. Countless friends and acquaintances can tell me what a kind man he is and how lucky I am to be married to someone who wants me to achieve the dreams I have. Yet, until something happens that drops me to my knees in prayer out of fear and helplessness—I take him and his love for granted.

Why is that?

Perhaps familiarity does breed a type of contempt.

But I don't want to live there—in a contemptuous relationship in which it takes a tragedy to soften my everyday emotions! I want to see my husband with 20/20 clarity. Knowing that the hours, days, months, and years that we have as man and wife are a gift—an incomprehensible gift from God that is intended to draw us closer to the Father of us both and to make us more like His Son, Jesus Christ.

What an incredibly difficult lesson to learn. And each time these horrific moments occur in the world I beg God, "Please, oh please, let me get it this time. And help me to see, truly see, how incredibly blessed and rich I am."

12

All I Need

Confession time again.

I love insanely stupid, sophomoric movies. And I love watching them with juvenile-adult friends, such as my best buddy from college, Audrey Denney Reischauer. The first movie of this genre that I watched with her was *Top Secret*. We were all of 18 at the time. The best thing about the entire evening was sitting next to Aud as she laughed through each scene.

See, my pal Audrey doesn't titter with laughter.

Nor does she guffaw or chortle.

My buddy is a noun unto herself—that is, laughing like an "Audrey." When she laughs, she *laughs*—really loud and until tears come down her face. And of course, I'm right in there crying and snorting with her because her laugh just makes me feel good.

It's like hearing that familiar voice from your past that makes you get all warm and fuzzy inside and makes you glad to be alive. That's what Aud's laugh is for me—a welcoming and at-home feeling of togetherness. Whether we're watching *Waterboy* or listening to some hilarious speaker at a women's conference, her robust and raucous laugh tops my list of things that are perfect in this world.

Making a Determination

So with that in mind, you'll appreciate my love for a classic scene from a popular Steve Martin film of the late '70s.

Upon losing all his riches and receiving an eviction notice, the main character, named Navel Johnson, begins to walk out of the house, making a speech about how little he really needs to be happy. He grabs a chair and declares, "That's all I need." But with each step he finds one more thing. "All I need to be happy is this chair, and that picture, and these glasses, and that rug, and these books, that's all I need!" Step by step, need by need, "stuff" by "stuff"— until pretty soon he is struggling even to walk beneath the "all-I-need-for-happiness" weight.

I love that scene. I'm pretty certain that the writers of the movie *The Jerk* were simply going for the laughs, but I've found it to be a rather poignant reminder of my frail humanity.

For you see, the "spiritual author" side of me wants to say to you, "All *I* really need is the Lord, that's all I need." But I can't say it. I simply can't—because in all likelihood after I'd declared such profundities you'd probably see me grabbing a Coach purse or a three-stone diamond ring on my way out the door of "all I need"! And I'm not alone— after all, you'll recall author Dave Meurer and his take on the matter in chapter 4!

So let's get honest here. The trick is to be truthful and forthright when considering the "all I need" details of life.

Defining "all I need" takes a lot of thought, and I'd humbly suggest that you include a prayer or two—as you desire to learn what really matters most in our marriage and in our lives.

Just Gotta Have It!

In a random survey the following were mentioned as being absolute needs in life:

- a puppy's warm belly to rub

- a bowl of spicy hot chili on a cold December night

- the experience of being kissed by an open-mouthed, drooling toddler

- watching your adult parents dance to the sounds of a big band

- listening to your child pray, "Jesus, please come into my heart"

- smelling the aroma of baking bread as you enter your grandma's house

- catching a big fish—without any help

- hearing your baby's heartbeat at 16 weeks and then watching as your wife pushes that little one out into the world five months later

- finding a dozen red roses waiting for you after a long day at work

- making love with the one you have vowed your life to

What Say Ye?

If you only had five minutes to gather up the important things in your home (besides the members of your family)—what would they be?

Photos?

A cardboard box full of legal yellow pads with years' worth of ramblings and writing ideas?

A certain piece of jewelry?

A treasured Bible?

No matter—those things that you would go for *first* are those that are truly important to you. So take the time to embrace them *now*. To enjoy the people that bring you joy. To peruse photographs and revel in the memories they stir up. And wear the jewelry now—don't worry about "saving it for good."

Debtly sinning obscures the here and now—the "all we really need" reality of life, marriage, and satisfying relationships with one another. I've found, much as shown by the list of needs above, that my most basic needs most often come down to flesh-and-blood interactions with those I love.

I absolutely need to feel Rick's warm embrace and to hear him whisper, "I'm still crazy about you, Julie."

I absolutely need to know that there is one man on the face of this planet who is faithfully committed to me.

And I absolutely need to be needed. Which so wonderfully meets the bare-bones needs of my husband.

Rick needs to be welcomed after a long day with a playful peck to his cheek and a "meet me later, baby!" look in his wife's eyes.

He needs to know that there is one woman on the face of this planet who is faithfully committed to him.

And he absolutely needs to be the sun, the moon, and the stars in someone's world.

And he is.

There are material things that he and I both need. I, a dishwasher. He, a Sawzall that cuts through drywall and steel pipe! But more than anything else we need each other. One financial loser lovin' another financial loser…all the way to the very end.

Debtly Sin #6
Regret

13

Shoulda, Woulda, Coulda

The perilous temptation to look back over one's life with agonizing regret is a debtly sin that most 30-something adults can relate to. (As well as 20-somethings, 40-year-olds, and those in their 50s, 60s, and older! Regret is no respecter of age.)

I've heard Rick lament time and time again, "I should have gone ahead and completed my four-year degree!" Especially these last few months, after losing, as a result of corporate downsizing, his human-resources position and finding himself enrolled in a four-year degree program at our local Illinois University—at age 36. And I have repeatedly commented since graduating college in 1987, "Why didn't I go on and get my master's degree?"

What *were* we thinking?

Despite my passion for books and intellectual discussion and Rick's love for anything pertaining to athletics, neither of us zealously pursued an academic or sports career. We simply went to college, fell in love, dated one another four years, and then got married.

In 1987, after Rick had received an associate degree in criminal justice and I had graduated with a bachelor of science degree in elementary education, we married. Okay, it wasn't quite that neat and tidy—or simpleminded! But in hindsight it's quite easy to see that both he and I opted for the "traditional"—if not "easy"—way of life. Without too much effort we found ourselves married to someone we were crazy about, employed, and eager to enjoy the days and nights ahead as man and wife.

Little did we know that just a few short weeks later we would be faced with the first of several "shoulda" moments that would impact both our marital and financial relationship.

We Shoulda "Expected the Unexpected"

First, let me say that our first child, Kristen, knows she was absolutely loved the moment her presence was known.

There were no regrets as we looked at the blue "YOU'RE PREGNANT!" test stick and no regrets as I watched my belly button stretch to widths unknown to womankind! (Okay, Rick may have regretted that just a little, but Kristen shouldn't take that personally.) And there wasn't a single regretful moment in our birthing room as we finally held her—14 hours after labor had begun.

None.

We counted each finger and each exquisite toe—basking in the aroma of our newborn child.

But...Rick and I had not *planned* on conceiving a child on our honeymoon night. We had all those plans that I told you about in chapter 4! Plans for making money. Plans for spending all the money we were going to make. And plans to just "be."

To be an up-and-coming couple of substance and wealth, thank you very much.

Well, you know what they say God does when you tell Him all your plans, don't you? He laughs. Not a snide laugh, but a tender, Father-like laugh that says "Just wait and see what I have in store for you!"

So several weeks after our honeymoon I found myself "with child." Suddenly the thrill of bringing home a paycheck and contributing to society as a teacher didn't seem that important. All I could think of and all I wanted to do was to be able to stay home with my baby after she was born.

And Rick, who up until that moment had made his plans for our future based on two incomes, was now faced with the daunting task of providing for Kristen and me on his small salary alone. He quickly realized (with the first bit of debtly regret) that he shoulda thought a bit more carefully concerning his education and the earning potential a four-year degree afforded over a two-year.

Sigh.

Shoulda, coulda, woulda…didn't.

We Shoulda Saved for an Emergency

Three weeks after Kristen's birth, we moved to Greenville, Mississippi.

In response to our surprise baby, Rick had interviewed for a promotion in the Loss Prevention Division of Wal-Mart. Unfortunately, it was not possible to remain in our college hometown, and we found ourselves packing and preparing for a move to a place 13 hours away from family and friends.

On a warm fall morning, Rick and my father led a "Mississippi or Bust" convoy to our new destination. The Ryder truck held all our worldly goods as well as pulling our "pre-baby" hatchback car. My grandmother rode with Kristen and me in our new "family sedan" while my mother brought up the rear in a vehicle to return home in.

After a tearful goodbye three days later, Rick and I were left alone with our tiny baby girl. I was ready to play house and see Rick succeed at his new job. Making our small apartment homey and welcoming for Rick and the new friends that we were meeting at the church we attended kept me busy. As well as taking care of Kristen and reveling in the time we spent together as mother and daughter.

But...homemaking and entertaining don't come cheap.

So in an effort to entertain and show hospitality in the manner I'd always dreamed, I began charging lots of items to our credit card.

Forest-green mats for the bathroom.

Brass wall sconces for the small living room.

Kitchen gadgets for deveining shrimp (which are a cheap commodity in Mississippi for some reason!).

Baby gyms and bedding for Miss Kristen, and a few larger-size pants for me.

Seems I had discovered the Krispy Kreme equivalent of yeast doughnuts in Greenville: Shipley Doughnuts. Doughnuts—as in homemade, yeast-risen, glaze-covered, cooked-to-perfection doughnuts! Every morning Kristen and I would drive half a mile from our apartment building and purchase three or four. Sometimes I charged them— pathetic carb lover that I am!

And so this pattern continued. Rick off to work, Kristen and I left to our own female devices—spending money with nary a thought and trying to fill the ache of homesickness with stuff and doughnuts. I took no note of the future or of what *could* be, and that's where February 14, 1988, found us.

Rick left the house exceptionally early that morning, around 4:30 A.M., and unlike most times, I walked with him to the front door and kissed him goodbye. I also prayed very specifically for his safety that morning. I can remember the exact words I said as he backed up our blue Buick Century and disappeared down Beauchamp Avenue.

"Dear God, I ask that you would place your angels in front of Rick, behind Rick, to the left and to the right of Rick, and beneath Rick."

I returned to bed and immediately fell back to sleep.

A couple of hours later I had just given Kristen her first morning bottle when the phone rang.

"Hello, is this Mrs. Rick Barnhill?"

"Yes, it is."

"Please hold, ma'am, your husband would like to speak with you."

I had no idea what was going on. Then I heard Rick's voice.

"Hey, hon, it's me."

"Rick, are you okay?"

"Well, I was in a car wreck and I think I broke my leg, but I'm okay."

What? How could he have been in a car wreck when he was supposed to be in West Helena, Arkansas?

"Rick, where are you?"

I overhead him talking with someone—wherever it was he was at.

"Hon, I'm going to have to let you talk with the nurse here, she'll tell you where I am."

"Wait! Rick! Are you hurt bad? I need to know if you're okay!"

"Julie, I am okay, I just need you to talk to the nurse right now. Here she is."

And with that he turned me over to the emergency-room nurse in charge of his care.

"Hello, Mrs. Barnhill?"

"Yes, it's me—please tell me, what happened to my husband?"

"Mrs. Barnhill, he was involved in a head-on collision near Gunnison, Mississippi. I am calling you from Cleveland, Mississippi—where he was first transported from the scene of the accident—and we are preparing him for further transport to Greenwood Leflore Hospital in a few minutes, ma'am."

My mind was reeling at this point. Where was Cleveland, Mississippi? Where for that matter was Greenwood, Mississippi? As Kristen lay sleeping, her father was somewhere far away from me and in great pain—I could hear it in his voice though he tried to mask it the best he could.

"I need to know what his exact injuries are."

"Ma'am, he has a compound fracture to the right knee, a crushed right foot, lacerations to the chest, rib cage, and face, as well as a torn rotator cuff."

I couldn't make sense of what she was telling me. She reeled the items of as though reciting a grocery list.

"Wait a minute, you said compound fracture to his right knee. Isn't that when the bone pierces the skin?" Thoughts of infection and the threat of gangrene filled my mind as I realized that Rick, in all likelihood, had been lying injured beside a dirty and wet roadside.

The nurse interrupted my worries with her answer.

"No, ma'am."

Did she just say "No, ma'am"?

I begged to differ. "Huh, yes it is," I argued. "A compound fracture is a piercing of the skin by bone." I then quoted from the medical reference book I had grabbed off our stacked bookshelves.

"Well, I don't know about that, ma'am. All I can tell you is, he'll be arriving at Greenwood Leflore Hospital in the emergency room in just a little over an hour. I'm sure the doctor will be able to tell you all about his injuries there."

What kind of nurse was this? I asked to speak once more with Rick. However he was unable to talk to me because of the pain of his injuries. I then instructed the nurse to tell my husband I would be at the hospital as soon as I found a place for Kristen to stay.

Hanging up the phone, I realized—we had never prepared for something like this.

Did we have a savings account we could fall back on? No.

Had we purchased the highest amount of uninsured-motorist protection from our insurance agent? No.

Were our monthly expenses well within our means? No.

Would we be able to meet the minimum payments due to our creditors on a reduced disability check? Never.

Debtly regret after debtly regret came to mind as I sped the 52 miles to Greenwood. And as I steeled myself mentally for the possibility of any life-threatening or disabling injuries my husband might have suffered, I simply could not see any hope in our financial situation. All I could think of, over and over again, was this: *How on earth are we going to deal with this?*

14

Letting Go

Erma Bombeck, best-selling author and humorist of the 1970s and 1980s, wrote one of her most poignant and well-received newspaper columns during the last months she was battling kidney cancer.

"If I Had My Life to Live Over Again" she titled it, and then she shared with millions of faithful fans the regrets of her own life. I've read her words time and time again and am struck by the simplicity of what she wrote. From eating popcorn in the "good" living room (any child of the '60s and '70s can relate to that parenting no-no!) to speaking words of love and apology more often, Erma summarized the angst of looking back.

So many times—dare I say most times—it's not the great choices that eat away at our heart and spirit, but rather the simple things. The simple choices we could have so easily made—but didn't. And it is the simple things that pile up on one another, day after day, month after month, year after year, until finally one is left looking back— longing for the chance to do it all over again.

Erma's words confirmed to her public that—despite our fame, fortune, or standing in life—in the end we all look for and long for what is eternal. We want to believe that our lives have counted for something. We want to believe that we have squeezed out the last drop of life from the days we were given. And in the stillness of our souls and the far recesses of our memories, we long to believe that the choices we have made in the few earthly years we've been granted are indeed right and good.

The urge to "look back" and struggle with regret speaks to the nature of frail humanity (that would include you and me).

With or without a diagnosis of cancer, or a car accident that shakes your long-term plans, I think we all reach a point in our lives when we have to decide *what* we're going to do with our many regrets.

I suppose you could carry this emotional baggage for your entire life if you so chose. But I believe it's far better to recognize the shouldas and couldas and wouldas for their unflattering and painful selves and then use them as catalysts for change. I like to tell the audiences which I speak before this important truth: "As long as you're breathing, it's never too late."

No, it's never too late to attempt a "do-over."

It's never too late to learn from mistakes.

It's never too late to say, "I really messed up."

And it's never too late to make amends.

The Power of Released Regret

I could share innumerable moments with you. One after another, year after year, Rick and I came face-to-face with regrets of every kind.

I wish I could tell you that we learned immediately from the two debtly regrets we battled in the chapter before. But really, we didn't, though Rick did recover from his injuries. After all, it wasn't until a job loss in the fall of 2001 that Rick dealt seriously with his regrets regarding a four-year college degree. And me? Well, it took me eight years before I saw the error of my ways regarding credit-card charges and high-fat items like doughnuts and double-doozie cookies!

But if there is any hope to be found in our regretful wanderings it is this. At some indefinite point we both learned to get over it and to get on with it! Arthur Brisbane said, "Regret for time wasted can become a power for good in the time that remains. And the time that remains is time enough, if we will only stop the wasteful and idle useless regretting."

And that's what debtly regret is.

Useless—

Entirely pointless and without purpose unless we use it to spark a change in our thinking, our actions, and our planning. Regret alone neither lengthens your days nor increases your checkbook balance. It is regret finally released—let go and then coupled with active *desired* change—that makes our lives different.

God Will Reveal More of Himself

In the late 1980s two therapists named Arthur Freeman and Rose DeWolf authored a book they called *Woulda, Coulda, Shoulda: Overcoming Regrets, Mistakes and Missed Opportunities*. They looked at two questions: 1) What prevents us from doing what we would, could, and should do?

2) How do we deal with those woulda, coulda, and shoulda moments in our lives and the feelings of guilt and despair?

The challenge, they believed, was to learn how to avoid letting past couldas, wouldas, and shouldas so overwhelm us that it becomes impossible for us to act with an eye toward a future full of "cans," "wills," and "shalls."

Eureka! That is exactly what we have to do with the debtly sin of regret! We have to *confess* those regrets and then *use* them as an impetus—as a motivator—to do something different.

Look, all of us have regrets—I don't think any self-respecting human being can possibly *not!* Still, at some point we will either have to choose to seek freedom from their debtly grip or continue in the bondage in which they hold our past and our future.

I prefer freedom, and I have found the following three steps imperative in attaining this status:

1. We must own up to the regret itself and express it aloud. There's just something about confessing our sins aloud that brings freedom and release to our soul. It wasn't until I confessed aloud—both to Rick and myself—my sin of lying that I truly sensed a release from its weight.

2. After confessing the regret that has tied us up in guilty knots, we must acknowledge the harm it has brought into our marriage relationship. Acknowledge it, confess it, and then turn from its hold. And then (this is of utmost importance!)…

3. We must ask God to mature our shallow faith (for immature faith often causes us to hesitate to move on dreams He's given us, or to cling to the things that money buys!). Ask that He move you "higher up, and deeper in," as C.S. Lewis once wrote. We were created by One who finds no greater pleasure than that of showing us more of Himself.

For right there—in the midst of our confession, in our acknowledging of regret's death grip on our lives, and in our bold request for a deeper faith that no longer doubts and tries to fill the soul with stuff-mart items—He can forgive and release you from the shouldas, couldas, and wouldas of a lifetime!

Debtly Sin #7

Giving Up

15

Exit, Stage Left

I never thought I would leave my marriage.

As I repeated my vows on a cold December evening in 1987, I meant every word I said. I had chosen to marry Rick, and I desired nothing less than God's absolute blessing upon our life as man and wife. During the ceremony, Rick and I pledged to honor and love one another, to share all our material possessions with one another, and to have our sexual needs met solely within the confines of our marriage relationship.

We also spoke words from the Song of Solomon—Rick quoting chapter 4, verse 9, "You have stolen my heart...my bride, you have stolen my heart"—and I, chapter 5, verse 16, "This is my beloved and this is my friend."

Like thousands of men and women before us we vowed to remain with one another until death alone parted us. Again, I meant every word, and I never thought I would contemplate going back on the promises I had made before Rick, God, and 300-plus witnesses.

But I did.

In 1997, while lying next to my husband in our darkened bedroom (but feeling as though he were a million miles away), I was faced with answering this question: *Am I going to stay in this marriage?*

Notice I did not ask, *Do I want to stay in this marriage?* Because quite frankly the answer was *no*—I was ready to quit.

You see, we had been riding the roller coaster of Chronic Financial Failure for more than five years! Climbing to dizzying heights of unsecured borrowing, we would then plummet and hit upon the costly reality of having jumped carelessly aboard—time and time again.

We both knew that something was wrong. Yet neither one of us was willing to tackle the glaring problems within our marriage. "Don't ask, don't tell" had borne its ugly fruit. Our finances were a joke, and our lovemaking—which had always been the one safe and satisfying place we could go—had all but disappeared. Truth was, we were living more as distant friends than as man and wife. And the reality that we could be lying next to one another in our bed and have absolutely nothing to say to one another was absolutely devastating to my soul.

So on that particular evening in 1997, I spoke into the darkness.

"Rick, if we don't deal with what's going on in this marriage my heart is going to continue to harden against you. And even though I may not leave you physically, I will shut you off emotionally."

And then in the faintest whisper, "I'm afraid I already have."

This was how I found myself after playing financial roulette with our money and marriage—an emotionally bankrupt woman, contemplating physical separation, and even divorce, as a means of getting away from financial trouble and regrets.

The Answer to the Mess

Somewhere between "I do" and "I want out," walls of separation can systematically destroy the intimacy that every long-term and healthy relationship needs. And it is my belief that those walls are built from and supported by the debtly sins we tolerate and practice in our marriage.

As a reader, you need look no further than the painful examples Rick and I have chosen to share with you—or perhaps no further than your own marriage.

In our case, with each lie I spoke, I was destroying trust and intimacy with Rick.

With each unrealistic expectation that he refused to budge on, our marriage suffered the consequences.

One by one—from unrealistic expectations to "exiting stage left"—sin hardened our hearts and laid the groundwork for our marriage's failure.

I believe it's time we faced the truth and faced up to this fact: the *'Til Debt Do Us Part* issues of our marriage will be resolved not when we have more money, but when we have acknowledged and relinquished the debtly habits, motives, thoughts, and attitudes that we hold on to as husbands and wives.

And I'll boldly tell you this—you will not be able to accomplish this by your own strength and power. Trust me again, I've made more resolutions, bought more budget books, and felt more guilt than most people can ever imagine!

But none of it stuck.

It wasn't until I called my deeds *sinful* and began to pray this prayer: "Lord, show me what's wrong with me," that I was able to sense a softening in my heart toward Rick. It wasn't until I confessed, "God, I want to think differently about money and stuff…but I can't," that I recognized my weakness and embraced it. Embraced it as He gently reminded me, "Without Me you can do nothing."

And that's the truth.

You and I cannot do this marriage thing. Alone.

We cannot rein in our wants and desires. Alone.

We cannot let go of our selfishness. Alone.

We are a mess. Alone.

But with Him—

You and your husband—you and your wife—can love one another and experience intimacy and companionship like never before. With Him.

You can gain self-control and learn contentment. With Him.

You can let go of yourself and learn to live for others—for your spouse. With Him.

We are a mess. But with Him we are made right.

16

A Covenant Commitment

When you first got married, what were you expecting from your relationship?

Did you marry to find physical, financial, or emotional security?

Did you marry to escape your parents' home?

Or perhaps were you in love with the notion of waking up next to someone day after day, someone who enjoyed and desired your companionship? Whatever our reasons or motives, more than a few of us bring to marriage a contract-like list of things that will be done or not done. Do's and don'ts, needs and wants, that will ensure the happiness and longevity of the marriage.

I like to refer to these as our "terms of engagement."

"Terms of engagement" are quite simply this: the rules, conditions, and principles by which we gauge our marriage's success or failure. Though occasionally opinioned aloud, most often our terms of engagement are silent bargaining tools by which we judge our spouse's commitment, our marriage's viability, or our own happiness within that relationship.

These terms are based on the mindset that marriage is in fact a contractual agreement between a man and woman. You scratch my back, I'll scratch yours, so to speak. Let me give you three simple examples.

Term of Engagement # 1:

One's duty to follow through with the marital commitment is based on the compliance of the other person to certain rules and conditions.

For instance, I promised to love Rick through all manner of good and bad. I spoke vows that covered better and worse, richer and poorer, and sickness and health. But oftentimes I applied my contractual terms of engagement, and in essence acted as if I had really said "I will love you if you love me," or "I will put up with the worst as long as I know you're actually doing something to change it!"

Term of Engagement #2:

Failure to comply releases the other party from the agreement.

In short, this term communicates, "Hey, you didn't keep your end of the bargain so I don't have to either." I've heard that very statement from the lips of hurt and frustrated spouses. "Julie," one broken woman told me, "he knows we're supposed to discuss all major purchases with one another. He knows I worry about our financial security and I stay up late thinking about it. But he can't seem to keep his end of the agreement…and once again I'm dealing with the consequences of his stupid and thoughtless behavior!" (Here comes the kicker.) "So I figure, if he hasn't been honest with me, I don't have to be honest with him."

Term of Engagement #3:

Marriages are over when promises are broken.

In the all-or-nothing world of contractlike marriages there is little room for failure or mistakes. Our terms of engagement override the vows of "forever and ever, amen." With black-and-white clarity we say to the offending spouse, "You did not fulfill your end of the deal, our contract is broken." Or as game-show host Ann Robinson might say, "You are the weakest link, goodbye!"

Grace is a rare commodity in the terms listed above. So it should come as no surprise when we see marriage after marriage faltering beneath their crushing weight. I can tell you this from personal experience and from watching the devastating aftermath of the collapse of relationships built upon a contract of expectations—your marriage will not thrive, and in all likelihood will not survive, in such a graceless atmosphere.

A Covenant Concept

This is almost too embarrassing to admit—but considering all I've written previous to this chapter, I think I'll go ahead. It wasn't until the summer of 2001 that I ever heard of the concept of marriage being anything *but* a contractual agreement! I had bought into the "it's all about me" mentality that many in my generation have believed. So it was with a raised eyebrow and piqued interest that I ran upon a live radio broadcast out of Chicago.

Rick and I were working on a remodel of the upstairs bathroom of our home. Hoping to tune into our favorite "best of the '70s and '80s" radio program, I began scanning for the station that carried it. That's when I happened upon the welcoming voice of Dennis Rainey, who was leading the opening session of the one-day marriage conference, "I Still Do." For the next three hours or so, while Rick and I painted ceiling molding and hung faux-wainscoting wallpaper, we listened as the biblical concept of marriage being a *covenant* relationship was presented by various speakers. Presented to us for the very first time.

I was completely mesmerized by the teaching, and by the end of the afternoon Rick and I both knew we had discovered the foundational truth that we could continue building our marriage upon. At last we understood that the power of our marriage vows lay in a much deeper and more supernatural reality than we had ever considered.

It wasn't a contract that we had entered into when we had signed our wedding license in 1987. Rather it was a *covenant agreement*—an irrevocable pledge of faithfulness and commitment to one another, an expression and reflection of God's faithful commitment to us. Marriage was never designed to function as a contract, which depends upon a man or woman's ability to meet standards and requirements. Rather, it was designed to be a binding agreement between two or more people—you, your spouse— and God. The Designer Himself said, "'A man shall leave his father and mother and be joined to his wife, and the two shall become one flesh'...So then, they are no longer two but one flesh. Therefore what God has joined together, let not man separate" (Matthew 19:5-6 NKJV).

And then going one step further He tells us that our ability to see this covenant through to the very end will not depend on our faithfulness but on His! God says to you and me, "You can love this man or woman for a lifetime because I have loved you with an everlasting love!" In short, when we begin to live and love in line with the covenant truth of marriage we will be able to say, "Regardless of what you do or don't do, I will continue to love you."[12]

In an online interview, author Holly J. Lebowitz made this comment regarding marriage: "I don't have answers to what's taking marriage and families apart other than pointing people to God. We need someone bigger than ourselves to help us overcome our selfishness, because that's what's wrong with marriage today. I believe that if God designed marriage, he knows how to make it work."[13]

Amen to that!

Just Stand

Now, some of you are probably thinking, "But I can't commit myself like this. You don't understand the difficulties I'm experiencing in my marriage."

Hear me. Just stand.

Plant your feet on the foundational truth that this union with your spouse is built upon the Rock of Jesus Christ rather than a contractual agreement between a man, a woman, and a lawyer.

Just stand. Not seeking an easy way out—not avoiding the debtly issues and sins that have brought you to this place.

Just stand and hold to the covenantal truth—that God desires for you and your spouse to remain one until the day you draw your final breath.

The apostle Paul encourages us to do just this in the sixth chapter of Ephesians, verse 13: "Put on the full armor of God, so that when the day of evil comes you may be able to stand your ground, and after you have done everything, to stand" (NIV).

As we move into part two of this book you're going to discover something about doing that—how to stand in His faithfulness toward financial losers, and how to stand on the bedrock of marital counsel, the Holy Scriptures.

But first, before you do anything else I'd like you to put the book down and do something for me. If your spouse is close beside you or somewhere in your vicinity, go get them. Now do this one thing: Wrap your arms around them, lay a big ol' kiss on their lips, and as you do simply whisper a prayer of thanks to God for their warm presence. Ahhh! That just feels good, doesn't it?

All right, let's move straight ahead into part two: filing Chapter 13 Relief!

PART TWO

Chapter 13
Relief

17

A Very Good Place to Start

Well, someone has to say it, so it might as well be me.

I think all Chronic Financial Failures should seriously consider filing for relief. After all, most of us are "loaned out" at this stage of the game. Our relatives have caller ID to better avoid our phone messages, and they probably delete any e-mails that pop up unexpectedly too. We're in deep trouble, and no one knows it better than we ourselves!

We *know* that our debt-to-income ratio is pathetic.

We *know* we've lost the war—for we have seen the enemy and it has a credit card with our spouse's name on it!

And while there is a certain comfort in knowing you aren't the only financial loser on the face of the planet, that knowledge in and of itself isn't enough to settle the anxieties and cure the trouble that living as one has created.

Help Is on the Way

Bankruptcy is a legal process that allows financially distressed individuals to have some or all of their debt eliminated and enables debtors to get a "fresh start" on their finances. Call me crazy, but I think more than a few of us meet the criteria for filing such a motion.

We're distressed individuals.

We have a lot of debt that we'd love to see eliminated.

And there isn't a soul reading this book who wouldn't love the chance to get a fresh start on all things financial in his or her life!

(Are you still with me, or are you shaking your head wondering what type of advice I'm about to give next?)

Therefore, with these facts in mind, I propose that all financial losers file a voluntary petition for bankruptcy and seek relief for all their debt under Chapter 13 protection. But you need to know this one thing: Our petition won't be received in a federal court building or by an astute attorney-at-law.

For the Chapter 13 relief we seek won't be granted through legal wrangling but through the very Word of God—as found in the book of 1 Corinthians, chapter 13, verses 4 through 8.

We've tried everything else, so it's time to give up and turn over all our debt (financial, emotional, spiritual, marital) to the Judge who is able to grant us a fresh start! It is the uncompromising belief of this author and financial loser that, without a supernatural working of God *within* us, we will never be able to experience lasting and (dare we believe?) *joyful* change in our marriages, our checkbooks, and our future.

How can I make such a bold statement?

It's quite simple, really.

For more than ten years *I* did everything possible to overcome my financial tendencies. I even tried to overcome Rick's for him too! I read the books on money management.

I clipped coupons. (Okay, this was a very short-lived thing, but I did try!) I tithed. I didn't tithe. I felt guilty for not tithing and wrote a check when I knew it had a 99.9 percent chance of bouncing to the very gates of heaven! (Note: This a poor Christian witness!)

Rick and I attended weekend money seminars for couples, and the only consensus we ever came to was that I wrote far too many checks to the Sirloin Stockade!

We vowed to change our ways.

To keep one another accountable.

To "discuss" all purchases before the purchase.

We paid back parents and vowed never to borrow again.

And time and time again, we failed.

Healing from the Word

Then an amazing thing happened: I rediscovered the thirteenth chapter of 1 Corinthians!

Now I know that sounds rather *un*-amazing, but hear me out on this, please. I had read this familiar chapter time and time again. In fact, verses 4 through 8 were so marked up in my trusty New American Standard Bible that I decided to read instead from Eugene Peterson's contemporary-language edition, *The Message*.

The last thing on my mind at that time was the debtly condition of my heart—or anyone else's for that matter. I had long stopped expecting "manna" miracles and in fact had accepted that defeat was the nature of my marriage and my ways.

But it's right at that place where the "amazing" comes in!

As I skimmed over each of those familiar verses it was as if I were reading and hearing their message for the very first time. And over and over again, in that still quiet place of my heart I sensed His Spirit whisper—

"Live these words and prosper."

Okay, I saw that little red flag of warning pop up in your thinking! Allow me to clarify those whispered words before you erroneously assume that I am about to take back everything I said about cheesy Christian promoters and authors and hit you with some kind of deal.

My encounter with 1 Corinthians 13 had nothing to do with "name it and claim it" theology. Nor was I enlightened by some celestial message about coupon usage, budget guidelines, sock-darning as a second income, or once-a-year cooking tips! All of those are well and fine and do have their place in the discussion of debt and marriage, but this was something entirely different.

Five words—"live these words and prosper"—spoken as a gentle rebuke yet piercing my heart with boundless love and tenderness and opening my mind to the healing power of His Word.

Healing for my defeated soul.

Healing for my marriage.

Healing for a lying tongue and a wayward heart.

Healing from my Chronic Financial Failure.

And the incredible thing is, while I sensed He was correcting me as a parent must do, in all of that I never felt His rejection or embarrassed disappointment. I simply knew that my Father—the Judge of heaven and earth—had bent down and met me exactly where I was.

Broken.

Defeated.

Worn.

Once again—for He had used the same means to teach me the truth about my anger towards my children—it was His very Word, the Bible, that He chose as an instrument to bring about lasting change in my life and my needs.

With the same boldness that helped me confess my sin of monetary lying, I say to you now that, apart from our applying and living the radical truth of God's instructions and commands for us as believers, we will never experience change that lasts the course of our lifetime.

Financial tools and software will come and go.

Investment brokers will win and lose.

Corporate mergers will succeed and fail.

The economy will have its recessions and depressions.

But the Word of God and the love of the Father toward His children *are*—from everlasting to everlasting. And it is His *agape* love and the supernatural power of His written word to those who believe on Him that will empower and equip you to deal with all debtly sin.

I challenge you, dear financial loser: Consider the Scripture verses following. Meditate (plan, think deeply and continually) upon them as He instructs us to do. Pray that you may live—truly live out—each of the chapter 13 verses in your relationship as man and wife and as individual children of God. And above all, allow yourself to entrust yourself to a faithful Creator, and be prepared to give Him all the glory as you find relief, forgiveness, healing, and freedom!

A Meditation for Healing Hearts

"The tenderness and love of God our Savior has dawned in our lives; he saved us not because of any righteous deeds we had done but because of his mercy" (3:4-5 JB). We can embrace our whole life story in the knowledge that we have been graced and made more beautiful by the providences of our past history. All the wrong turns in the past, the detours, mistakes, moral lapses, everything that is irrevocably ugly or painful, melts and dissolves in the warm glow of accepted tenderness. As theologian Kevin O'Shea writes, "One rejoices in being unfrightened to be open to the healing presence, no matter what one might be or what one might have done."[14]

18

Love Is Patient

Relief from Money & Marriage Realities

Love, we are told in verses 4 through 8 of 1 Corinthians 13, is demonstrated through action.

We may have talked a good talk or even pledged ourselves to grandiose schemes, but genuine love for one another, God, and even ourselves is evidenced in the outward working of thoughts and intentions. That is why—as I read each succinct word of these verses—I tremble. I tremble with an odd mix of fear and anticipation, for I know I have fallen short of their holy charge again and again. Yet there resides within me a steely resolve, a passionate longing to weave this truth into the details of my life and my relationship with my husband.

I Want to Know What Love Is

Our culture revolves around the notion of romantic love. From the moment you turn on the radio, begin watching a romantic movie, or read your first Danielle Steel novel, you're inundated with phrases proclaiming—

I'm in love.

I think I'm falling in love.

I'm hopelessly in love.

I'm addicted to love.

But ask for a definitive meaning of this much-bandied-about word, and you'll soon find yourself lost in a fog bank of opinions. "Love is the conscious attraction to good," the great philosopher Aristotle believed. "Love stinks!" sang the J. Geils Band in the 1980s. "Love is when you go out to eat and give someone most of your french fries without making them give you any of theirs," declares a five-year-old.

And while these quotations are interesting and one could fill page after page with such opinions, in the end we are still left asking, "What is love?"

Love, True Love

Paul, in 1 Corinthians,* speaks of love as a noun. The *Matthew Henry Commentary* notes that love—*agape* (pronounced "ah-GAH-pay") in the original Greek of the New Testament—is "in its fullest and most extensive meaning, true love to God and man, a benevolent disposition of mind towards our fellow-Christians, growing out of sincere and fervent devotion to God. This living principle of all duty and obedience is the more excellent way of which the apostle Paul speaks."[15]

---

* The divinely inspired author of 1 Corinthians was the apostle Paul. This is the same man who, until his dramatic encounter with Jesus on a road leading to the city of Damascus, passionately pursued and persecuted those who followed Him. But he who had once hated and vilified the church of Christ was radically changed by the love of Christ. I think it's important to remember these facts about Paul, as they lend great credibility to the life-changing, transforming power of love. All this should encourage us as we desire transforming change in our financial mindsets and marriage.

Paul understood *agape* love to be a characteristic word of Christianity. *Agape* identifies us as followers of Christ. *Agape* is

> able to endure evil, injury, and provocation, without being filled with resentment, indignation, or revenge. It makes the mind firm, gives it power over the angry passions, and furnishes it with a persevering patience, that shall rather wait and wish for the reformation of a brother than fly out in resentment of his conduct. It will put up with many slights and neglects from the person it loves, and wait long to see the kindly effects of such patience on him.[16]

Agape is our lifestyle! We are motivated to act by the divine love that Christ demonstrated toward us and that the Father continues to express to His creation!

So in the end we learn that love—true love—isn't a sappy line in a greeting card or an emotion that we manipulate at will. Love—*agape* love—is a possessive noun that permeates every fiber of our being and lays claim to every relationship in our lives. It is a love that reconfigures our wants and desires and bears testimony to the One who first loved us! God desires *agape* to be the characteristic word of our lives—and then out of its abundance will flow the words, actions, and motives that we, as debtly sinners, have considered all but impossible!

Good News

We can celebrate not only our release from specific debtly sins but this marvelous truth also: God has *never* considered bailing out on you and me!

His love is from everlasting to everlasting. His nature is *agape*—love that is *patient* and *never gives in*. And His Word promises us that He will remain our never-ending Source of *agape* as we purposefully extend mercy and grace towards our spouse and apply Chapter 13 relief to our debtly sinning.

Now, we need to allow this perfect love to reshape our marriage and finances. In the following chapters are practical suggestions and more Chapter 13 truths that can help you on your healing journey out of Chronic Financial Failure. Here are a few verses to start you off.

- In the book of Jeremiah, God speaks through the Old Testament prophet and declares, "I have loved you with an everlasting love; therefore I have drawn you with lovingkindness" (31:3).

- David reassures us in Psalm 37:23-25 that "the steps of a man are established by the LORD, and He delights in his way. When he falls, he will not be hurled headlong, because the LORD is the One who holds his hand. I have been young and now I am old, yet I have not seen the righteous forsaken or his descendants begging bread."

- David also speaks of God's faithful presence: "'I love You, O LORD, my strength.' The LORD is my rock and my fortress and my deliverer, my God, my rock, in whom I take refuge; my shield and the horn of my salvation, my stronghold" (Psalm 18:1-2).

Be encouraged! You can start again—recommitting yourself to your spouse, your marriage, and your desire to be financially free! For *agape* never quits. Like the Energizer bunny, it just keeps going, and going, and going, and...

A Prayer for Your Marriage

"May the Lord bless you and sustain you, may the Lord pour the riches of His grace upon you, that you may please Him in body and spirit, and grow together in love all the days of your life."

∞

May they not expect that perfection of each other that belongs alone to Thee. May they minimize each other's weakness, be swift to praise and magnify each other's points of comeliness and strength, and see each other through a lover's kind and patient eyes.

Now make such assignments to them on the scroll of Thy Will as will bless them and develop their characters as they walk together. Give them enough tears to keep them tender, enough hurts to keep them humane, enough of failure to keep their hands clenched tightly in Thine, and enough success to make them sure they walk with God.

May they never take each other's love for granted, but always experience that breathless wonder that exclaims, "Out of all this world you have chosen me." When life is done and the sun is setting, may they be found, then as now, hand in hand, still thanking God for each other. May they serve Thee happily, faithfully, together, until at last one shall lay the other into the arms of God. This we ask through Jesus Christ, Great Lover of our souls. Amen.

—Traditional wedding prayer[17]

19

Love Isn't Always "Me First" (Ouch!)

Relief from Unrealistic Expectations

Time after time Chapter 13 truth comes nose-to-nose with my need to have things my way or no way!

Take the last helping of a favorite dinner dish, for instance.

Yes, I know that Rick has been working all day and has had the equivalent of a Hostess Twinkie and Mountain Dew for his lunchtime meal. Yes, I know that I snacked throughout the meal preparations and also cooked myself up a tasty cheeseburger on the grill over the noon hour. Yes, I know that my three children would probably like to have a bite of that final portion also.

But I want it.

And though in most instances I demurely pass on Rick's offer to "split it with you," inside I am really perturbed.

After all, I spent the time cooking and shopping for the ingredients. I'm the one who got the house in order and did countless loads of laundry during the day. I'm the one who rolled out the noodles, stuffed them full of ricotta and mozzarella cheese, and simmered the tomato sauce for eight hours plus. Humph—I deserved that leftover portion for tomorrow's lunch!

Now, I'm sure you've never been that shallow.

I'm positive that your "I don't want to think about you more than me!" moments have centered at least on something more profound than an Italian pasta dish!

Nevertheless, we've all been there at some point, and honestly, putting another person before you can be a real drag. That's why we need Chapter 13 *agape* in our lives! We'll never get our eyes off ourselves without its equipping and empowering us to do so.

Humility and Love

Remember the character Fonzie from the TV show *Happy Days?*

He was the cool dude wearing a leather jacket who, with a snap of a finger, could have a bevy of babes surrounding him. Everybody thought Fonzie was the greatest. But he had one flaw. He couldn't admit when he was wr...when he was wrrrr...when he was not right! He couldn't even *say* the "w" word. He'd stutter and stop, unwilling to admit he was wrong.

Fonzie had issues with humility!

Not only did he not want to admit he was wrong, he also didn't want to be perceived as being weak. And I'm thinking that some of us just might have a few Fonzie tendencies when it comes to thinking of others ahead of ourselves!

Philippians 2:3 tells us, "Do nothing from selfishness or empty conceit, but with humility of mind regard one another as more important than yourselves."

"Regard one another as more important." Hmmm, that flies square in the face of my setting impossible expectations for my husband! Let me share a "spiritual" example from my past.

It's Not You, It's Me

If you recall, in chapter 4 I listed a few of the expectations I had for my future husband before I was married. And while I wanted a man with good looks and such, the greatest expectation I held was that he would be a spiritual giant. No, not a Christian who stood nine feet tall! I'm referring to his abilities to speak on profound Christian issues, his biblical prowess, and a propensity for uttering long and soulful prayers.

Indeed, I had expectations—unrealistic and big!

Rick and I wed, and reality began.

For days and months I waited: waited for him to engage me in conversations of existential breadth and depth, waited for him to read the books I had bought him for his birthday and Christmas, waited for him to pray for a length of time greater than two minutes (yes, I was timing him!), and waited for him to meet the exacting standards and expectations I had predetermined as appropriate to a spiritual giant.

Guess what? It never happened. For close to nine years I selfishly clung to all my unrealistic spiritual expectations and judged Rick against them. For close to nine years I whined and cried and complained about his spiritual status, both to God and to any other disgruntled Christian wife I encountered. For close to nine years—until God had mercy on Rick's soul (he was getting pretty tired of it all by that point!) and dealt soundly with my arrogant and sinful ways.

You see, it wasn't wrong for me to desire great and wonderful spiritual things for Rick. But what was wrong was this: I never once thought about or prayed about what God might have in mind for Rick apart from my list of expectations. It never entered my "me first" mind that God might have a plan for Rick that was different from my checkpoints and standards. And I suspect that I'm not the only spouse who's done this.

Do You Want to Become Great?

Here's what we must grasp. Without the spirit of humility infilling our motives and deeds we will succumb to self-motivated dreaming and scheming and will ineffectively express *agape* love to one another.

The only real way to take your eyes off yourself is to put them on someone else. And there are effective ways to do this. First, start by praying. It seems like this should be the easiest thing to do as Christian husbands and wives—but you know what? It's not. Oftentimes we simply don't "feel" like praying for the one who annoys us more than anyone else on the face of the earth. Sometimes we don't "feel" like bowing on our knees and praying because we know, no matter how hard we try to avoid it, we will always have to consider "our" heart and "our" intentions and "our" selfish motives. All which leads to our praying, "God, change *me*." (And people with "it's all about me" tendencies find this quite difficult to do!)

Nevertheless, this is where we must start. Prayer can change things, for we are praying and communicating with the God of the universe, and His desire will always be to make us more like His selfless Son Jesus Christ. And then, when we at last put our eyes on Jesus rather than ourselves, the me-first tendencies can be released and done away with by the power of His Word.

Secondly, we can consider our spouse's interests. Hear me, now—I'm not saying that your man should drag you kicking and screaming to the deer stand he has set up 90 miles into the woods! But what if one particular morning—after you've watched him prepare his bow and purchase the scent—you offer to join him? Right there in the woods, 40 feet above the ground on a deer stand built for two. Can you imagine his surprise? I think you can. And granted, he may decline your gracious offer, but wouldn't it be great to think of participating in something he loves, rather than complaining about it?

And finally, we can simply learn to be last. Ahrrg, this is going to take some serious *agape* power to achieve! Yet, it is something we must do. Jesus states, in Matthew 20:26-28, "Whoever wants to become great among you must be your servant, and whoever wants to be first must be your slave—just as the Son of Man did not come to be served, but to serve, and to give his life as a ransom for many" (NIV). The only "cure" for me-first sinning is the *agape*-filled Word of God. Apply its truths to the debtly sins of your life and discover a changed life and a changed attitude.

A Prayer for Unselfishness

O Divine Master, grant that I may not so much seek to be consoled, as to console; to be understood, as to understand; to be loved, as to love; for it is in giving that we receive, it is in pardoning that we are pardoned, and it is in dying that we are born to eternal life. All because you in love gave yourself for us. Amen.

—attributed to Francis of Assisi

20

Love Takes Pleasure in the Flowering of Truth
Relief from Crafty Communications

Speak truth.

That's what I've been drilling into the heads of my three children for more than 13 years now. When I sense them beginning to "fudge" about the exact details of something, I say, "Speak truth." When they avoid eye-to-eye contact with me and nervously shift their feet, I say, "Speak truth." And when I get all shifty-eyed while discussing the probable contents of our mailbox, do you know what Rick says to me now? "Speak truth."

I can't really say that I have relished or pleasured in the truth being made known about my marriage and my finances. In fact, I have found it to be quite painful—and something I'd just as soon avoid. (Trust me on this. I sent more than one e-mail to my agent requesting that we return all contracts for this book and just pretend that I never came up with the idea. But he wouldn't let me.)

So I have been forced to recall the many lies that I did in fact tell over the past decade or so. And though I never want to return to those deceitful communications, I know that it will be His grace, His Word, and His power alone—enabling me to live the disciplined life that He has commanded—that will ultimately keep me from speaking deception and mistruth.

Fear of Disappointment

I've asked myself many times while writing these chapters, "Was the lying worth it?" And time and time again I answer, "No."

Prolonging the agony was far more painful than it would have been to simply be up-front in the very beginning of our downward spirals. Hindsight always helps—but I'm still amazed at my skewed thinking in those days.

I didn't want to tell my husband? I was afraid to. But what was I afraid of? His anger? No, I have never been in fear for my safety because of any outbursts of anger from Rick. As I shared with you previously, Rick doesn't really explode…he simmers.

So what was it? It's taken me a while, but I think I've figured it out.

I was ashamed of my behavior—and afraid of disappointing Rick. He had complete faith in me. He trusted me. And it would never have occurred to him that I might lie about anything! Confessing to Rick my sins of lying was the most painful thing I have ever had to do in our marriage. Yet I shudder to think where we would be now if I hadn't.

The Route to Intimacy

We will never know true marital intimacy until we allow truth to flourish in our marriage.

We can know the pleasures of lovemaking with our spouse; we can share life-changing moments such as childbirth, adoption, or the achievement of some longed-for goal. But if we are lying to one another—if we are allowing the shame of our actions to keep us from facing the ugly truth of our most secret sins—we are not experiencing the deepest of all intimacies.

Duke University professors Stanley Hauerwas and William Willimon made this observation in their book *Resident Aliens:* "Even in marriage between Christians, we meet as strangers unable to tell one another the truth. Yet Christians believe that nothing is more important in marriage than truthfulness. People often lie most readily in marriage. They know that nothing can kill the fires of passion quicker than truth."

That's what I feared more than anything if I were to confess my lying and crafty communications. I was terrified that Rick—upon discovering the true nature of my spending, thinking, fears, and worries—would want out of our marriage. I was afraid to tell him the truth, for I saw it as the ultimate act of intimacy and trust—and I could not bear the thought of his rejecting me.

The Truth Shall Set You Free

So how do we become honest communicators rather than crafty ones? Let's consider the following.

- *We must speak truth, the whole truth, and nothing but the truth, always.* Don't be surprised when you find this to be one of the most difficult and painful steps of Chapter 13 relief! After all, if this is your particular debtly sin you've probably been doing it for some time. But don't let that stop you from placing your foot firmly on this next "lily pad" of faith and Christian discipline. Robert C. Crosby challenges us: "As long as there are buried resentments, hidden doubts, concealed frustrations and covered-up wounds, there is little hope for intimacy in a marriage or parenting relationship. Choosing to be a truth teller is a daring step and the only one that really works. There is no way to be truly knit together in soul with people you love without learning how to tell them the truth." I long for the intimacy that truth telling brings, how about you?

- *We must keep our answers short and sweet.* "Let your 'Yes' be 'Yes,' and your 'No,' 'No,' anything beyond this comes from the evil one" (Matthew 5:37 NIV).

- *Let others hear the words "I'm sorry."* They are often the most difficult words to say but also the most needful. A marriage cannot withstand the storms of life if one or both spouses are unwilling to admit when they are wrong or when they have hurt each other. Your greatest strength as a couple is realized in your ability to admit your sins, your weaknesses, and your wrongdoings toward one another.

- *Be ready to ask, "Will you forgive me?"* We all know that uttering those four words can only happen after a whole lot of "me-first, I-was-right" thinking has been put away. When your spouse sincerely confesses and asks forgiveness, do not harden your heart and refuse to forgive.

A Prayer for a Truth-Filled Life

Lord, since I want no more darkness in my life, I renounce all trickery, all hypocrisy, and all falsehood. I embrace truth openly and am ready to walk in the light with all who are around me. Give me Your grace in this. Amen.

21

Love Trusts God Always
Relief from Trivial Pursuits

Rick and I have placed our confidence in a lot of different things in regard to money and marriage.

We've trusted in the power of Visa—it was going to take us where we wanted to be. However, bankruptcy court was never listed as one of the possible ports of call! We've trusted in income from future book sales and scheduled speaking engagements—only to have events canceled and see sales figures fall flat.*

The strong economy mailed Rick a letter stating "Your job has been eliminated"—and you've already heard my whining about automatic bank deposits in previous chapters. So, I guess the pertinent thing to ask at this point in the book is the following: "Have we learned anything about trust through all this?"

---

* Translation: Your "bestseller" is going for 99¢ at the local Book Nook

A Name You Can Trust

There's a Scripture verse tucked away in the twentieth Psalm, verse 7, which reads, "Some trust in chariots and some in horses, but we trust in the name of the LORD our God" (NIV).

Throughout history men and women have placed their trust in countless things that neither lasted nor proved sufficient. (If they haven't become obvious by now, my chariots and horses were mentioned under Debtly Sin #4: Trivial Pursuits.) However, in the second part of Psalm 20:7 the writer tells us what he *does* trust in—what he has found to be reliable and true. It is the Name of the Lord.

Here is what Rick and I have learned. If we are truly *agape* lovers of God and of one another, we will trust in His Name for all things concerning our finances, our marriage, and our lives. To be sure, we can trust Him and place all our confidence in Him simply because He *is*. But He knows we struggle as mere humans, and He has *proven* His trustworthiness over and over again to Rick and me, forgiving us when we've sinned, comforting us when we have lost hope, and blessing us financially in ways we could have never imagined. What an incredible anchor His Name can be for you, if you'll but trust Him to act in your life!

Out of the Pit

We are loved and cared for by a God too wonderful to comprehend! He tells us that He formed each one of us and knows us intimately. He is a God who created the very foundations of the world, placed the stars in the sky, and can hold the oceans in the palms of His hand. This God desires to help us, nurture us, and to be there for us. His love and His nature are represented in the names given to

Him in Scripture. He is the Alpha and Omega, the beginning and the end. He is a Wonderful Counselor and the Bright and Morning Star. We can trust in His names, for each one represents the character, strength, and provision that His presence provides. He is—

- Elohim—our Creator
- El Elyon—God most high
- El Roi—the God who sees
- El Shaddai—the all-sufficient One
- Adonai—the Lord
- Jehovah—the self-existent One
- Jehovah-jireh—the God who provides
- Jehovah-rapha—the God who heals all hearts and scarred lives
- Jehovah-nissi, the Lord our Banner—the God who leads you in and out of battle
- Jehovah-mekoddishkem—the God who sets you apart in your desire for more of Him
- Jehovah-shalom, your peace—the God who calms your worried and anxious thoughts
- And finally, Jehovah-raah, the Lord Shepherd—the God who leads you.

Who couldn't trust a God like that?

If Creator God Elohim can hold each molecule in place and keep the earth spinning in its correct orbit, then surely He can handle my $219 dental bill!

If El Roi, the God who sees, can number the hairs on my head, than surely He can help me keep track of my spending.

And if Jehovah-raah, the Lord Shepherd, knows each and every one of His sheep by name, than surely He knows me. And will continue to lead me if I will but love Him and trust Him.

We do not have to stay in the pit of debtly despair. There is hope in the Name of the Lord our God, and we can indeed entrust ourselves to our faithful Creator!

A Prayer for Trust

My God, let me know and love you, so that I may find my happiness in you. Since I cannot fully achieve this on earth, help me to improve daily until I may do so to the full. Enable me to know you ever more on earth, so that I may know you perfectly in heaven. Enable me to love you ever more on earth, so that I may love you perfectly in heaven. In that way my joy may be great on earth, and perfect with you in heaven.

O God of truth, grant me the happiness of heaven so that my joy may be full in accord with your promise. In the meantime let my mind dwell on that happiness, my tongue speak of it, my heart pine for it, my mouth pronounce it, my soul hunger for it, my flesh thirst for it, and my entire being desire it until I enter through death into the joy of my Lord forever. Amen.

—Saint Augustine of Hippo

22

Love Doesn't Want
What It Doesn't Have

Relief from Discontent

Contentment—ah, yes.

Contentment with who I am in this marriage relationship. Contentment with who my spouse is—and contentment with the wheres, whats, and how manys of life. If we say we love one another then we will be content with one another.

True love—*agape* love—is not contingent upon our acquiring some level of success or measuring up to some standard of worthiness. Rather, true marital love looks at the other and says, "Right here, right now, just as things are—this is enough."

When we are dealing with marital issues such as money and contentment, the primary focus of any Christian couple must be on finding peace with God and one another, whether in poverty or in wealth. If we can know peace within our souls and our marriage relationship we will posses a treasure that both kings and paupers have searched for since the beginning of time.

We all want a love that will last a lifetime. All we need sometimes is a nudge in the right direction.

Nudging Toward Contentment

The first thing we can do is simply give thanks for what we do have. Oh, I know you've heard this one before, but let's really do it this time. Let's "count our blessings, name them one by one." I'll start, and you can chime in anytime you'd like.

Lord Jesus, I want to thank You for—

My computer.

The photographs of family and friends taped around its monitor.

I want to thank You for the people in those photographs and all the incredible memories I have of them.

I thank You for a piano that my children can play.

Boxed cake mixes—because I am a lousy cake baker!

I thank You for the gift of faith. Faith that enables me to believe in You, a God I cannot see with my eyes or touch with my hands.

And I thank You for this man whom I call my husband. Thank You for the love that brought us together and the love that You can and will continue to give us—keeping us joined as one.

Okay, you're next.

Then after we've counted our blessings, we can rest in God's care. "God will take care of you" isn't just a line in a hymnbook, you know. It is truth. We can relax, let down our guard, and rest in Him. We don't have to keep one eye open—just in case. We don't have to "help God out"—just in case. We can rest—and let go of those things that will never bring joy, contentment, and rest to our marriages and souls.

And we can learn to "say when." My first inclination is to run through life screaming, "More! More! I want more!" But true contentment mandates a change in my perspective. As I look at the things I have and consider the spiritual and material wealth that He has lavished upon my life, I am struck by the mindlessness of wanting more. My cup is full! I can "say when" and still have more than I will ever need. It's time we called out "when" and settled into the riches of all we have been given!

A Prayer for Contentment

O God, open our hearts to all the gifts of today, even the burdens that You call us to bear, that we may not waste our lives searching for the joy that is found only in the day that we have. Amen.

23

Love Never Looks Back
Relief from Regret

Do you remember the story of Lot's wife?

I'll give you two hints. Morton and seasoning.

Ah! Now you remember. Lot's wife has the dubious distinction of being the one and only woman in recorded history to be turned into a pillar of salt. How lousy is that? One minute you're fleeing a burning city and the next—bam! You're a giant Popsicle for horses and camels alike!

In case you don't know the details of this story let me share the basic facts from Genesis 19 crisply and concisely. Here goes.

1. Lot and his wife (she's given no name in Scripture) live in a wicked city.

2. God decides to destroy said wicked city.

3. God sends angels to escort Lot and his wife out of said wicked city to safety.

187

4. Lot and his wife are commanded to flee the city.

5. Lot and his wife are commanded to keep their eyes straight ahead. God forbids them to look back at where they'd been.

6. Lot's wife looks back (you know it's going to get ugly).

7. Lot's wife is transformed into a literal figure of salt.

8. Lot keeps on walking.

Now, I'm no Bible scholar, but it seems to me that God puts a pretty high premium on keeping your eyes straight ahead.

And though I'll never understand this side of heaven why He chose to change Lot's wife into salt, I'm not about to argue with Elohim, the Creator. What I will do is this: I will learn from the fatal mistake this disobedient woman made and fix my eyes straight ahead in my own journey— the journey out of the debtly sin of regret.

Lessons to Live By

Looking back is dangerous. If you want to restore your bankrupt marriage the first thing you'll have to stop doing is "looking back" with regret on the past of that marriage. This is one of those topics that Christians *do not* like to talk about. But the fact is, many husbands and wives are playing a dangerous game of what I call Regret Roulette. Time and time again they replay "if only" scenarios in their minds. Wishing they could redo this or that, or longing to change their marriage partner altogether. It doesn't take a rocket scientist to figure out that this is not a healthy activity for Christian couples to participate in. Let me tell you something, just in case you've forgotten.

You made a commitment for life!

Whew, I know there are days you wake up and that reality kind of hits you like a ton of laundry, but it's true nonetheless. Which leads me to remind you of this...

You can't go back!

You have to follow through. The poignant reality of Lot's wife is this: She almost made it. She had been rescued from the teeming hordes of a wicked city. She had her husband by her side. She even had a heavenly escort exhorting her on. Yet just as safety was in sight—she hesitated.

Perhaps she remembered a best friend.

Or a treasured family heirloom that she'd never hold again.

Lot's wife may have been out of Sodom, but her heart was still there. A mountain loomed ahead of her, ready to shelter and protect her. Yet for one fatal moment she longed for the old life. She longed for things that had been.

You got to keep on keeping on. The author of the book of Hebrews encouraged Christian believers to fix their eyes upon the "author and finisher" of their faith (Hebrews 12:2 NKJV). Jesus Christ stressed the importance of looking forward in Luke 9:62: "No one, having put his hand to the plow, and looking back, is fit for the kingdom of God" (NKJV).

Fleeing Regret

Have you looked back after beginning the job of marriage? Have you found yourself nearly escaping from the form of debtly sinning that ties you down, only to be drawn back into its clutches? Have you played Regret Roulette?

I cannot tell a lie (besides, you've got a book full of examples right here in your hand)—I looked back more times than I can remember. Thank God that He stopped the salt thing with Lot's wife! I'm afraid I'd have been pillarized long before now.

Again and again I played Regret Roulette—spun the cylinder, pulled the trigger, and found myself flat on the ground, stuck again in looking back to what might have been, rather than fixing my eyes on what was. And all it brought me was misery and discontent. Make no mistake about it. We will suffer fatal results to our marriages if we don't hurry up and learn from Lot's wife! Let's flee regret's power and keep our eyes firmly fixed on the Author and Finisher of our faith—and upon the one we have pledged our lives to.

A Prayer for Those Who Harbor Regrets

Dear Father, I cannot let go of the past without Your help. All I can see is the things that could have been. All I can hear are all the words I should have said. And all I can hope for is another chance to get things right.

Help me to release all those things, to truly hand them over to You and forget them. Wipe my memory clean, and give me eyes and ears that are able to look upon and listen to today. In Christ's name I pray. Amen.

24

Love Keeps Going Until the End

Relief from Giving Up

Robert Browning writes, "Grow old with me! The best is yet to be."

So love finds me nearly 15 years into the journey of "'til death do us part." Anxious to experience the days and nights that lie ahead. Longing to nestle within the safety of Rick's protective arms. And ready, joyously ready, to face whatever comes our way.

I read Rick's expression as he speaks to me of vacation plans and of his "spiritual giant" faith about this book's message, and it tells me all I need to know. This man is in for the duration. He isn't looking for an easy way out, and he hasn't held any of my debtly sins against me! Truly, *agape* love has taken our hearts captive, and we are more committed to "forever" than we ever have been in our marriage.

Celebrate Forever!

One of the things that is sure to bring a smile to my face is reading the "Anniversary" section of our local newspaper. Week after week, I read about a man and a woman who remained faithful to their covenant pledge to one another. Two photos usually accompany the text. One taken at the altar of youth—an unblemished, wrinkle-free bride and groom, with just a hint of once-upon-a-time magic in their eyes. The other—and the one that compels me to gaze at it again and again—taken down the road of life, now showing faces kissed by age spots, wrinkled with laugh lines and worry; yet despite time and sorrow, joy and pain, I can still catch a hint of fairy-tale magic in the couple's eyes.

And so love should be.

Unquenched by tears or distance. Faithful and sure. Elizabeth Barrett Browning wrote of such forever love.

> How do I love thee? Let me count the ways.
> I love thee to the depth and breadth and height
> My soul can reach, when feeling out of sight
> For the end of Being and ideal Grace.
> I love thee to the level of everyday's
> Most quiet need, by sun and candlelight.
> I love thee freely, as men strive for right.
> I love thee purely, as they turn from praise.
> I love thee with the passion put to use
> In my old griefs, and with my childhood's faith.
> I love thee with a love I seemed to lose
> With my lost saints—I love with the breath,
> Smiles, tears, of all my life—and, if God choose,
> I shall but love thee better after death.

> —*Elizabeth Barrett Browning,*
> "A Wife to a Husband" [18]

Love That Will Not Let Me Go

It is intrinsic to our souls to know that there is more to this life than what we can see and taste, touch and control.

Love—*agape* love—can never be quenched, and it compels us to live a transcendent life, accomplishing acts of eternal significance and creating relationships that last a lifetime!

The apostle Paul knew of such love.

He encountered it in a blinding light.

He taught of its power in the book of 1 Corinthians.

And he prayed that each of us might comprehend the magnitude of it!

> I bow my knees before the Father, from whom every family in heaven and on earth derives its name, that He would grant you, according to the riches of His glory, to be strengthened with power through His Spirit in the inner man, so that Christ may dwell in your hearts through faith; and that you, being rooted and grounded in love *agape,* may be able to comprehend with all the saints what is the breadth and length and height and depth, and to know the love of Christ which surpasses knowledge, that you may be filled up to all the fullness of God.
>
> Now to Him who is able to do far more abundantly beyond all that we ask or think, according to the power that works within us, to Him be the glory in the church and in Christ Jesus to all generations forever and ever. Amen (Ephesians 3:14-21).

How apt to close this final chapter with the words of Brennan Manning. For if you'll recall the beginning of this book, it was Brennan who urged us to make our way home back to the Father, gently chiding us to stop looking at the mess we have made (and are!), and beckoning us to simply return home to the One who awaits the pleasure of our company.

And that we have done. Now he speaks of the unfath-omable love that Paul spoke of in Ephesians, and once again draws us to the *agape* truth of God.

> The love of God is simply unimaginable....Do you really hear what Paul is saying [in Ephesians 3:17-19]? Stretch, man, stretch! Let go of impoverished, circumscribed, and finite perceptions of God. The love of God is beyond all knowledge, beyond any-thing we can intellectualize or imagine. It is not a mild benevolence but a consuming fire. Jesus is so unbearably forgiving, so infinitely patient and so unendingly loving that He provides us with the resources we need to live lives of gracious response. "Glory be to Him whose power, working in us, can do infinitely more than we ask or imagine."[19]

Oh, dear reader, that is the deep, deep love of Jesus toward us. Unbearably forgiving. Infinitely patient and unendingly loving! He loves us—reformed financial losers or still-getting-by debtly sinners. He loves us, and as we surrender our souls to His *agape* power the weight of sins past will fall off us and the memory of sin's consequences will fade. Truly, we have been "seized by the power of a great affection"—may that power consume our hearts as man and wife and bring honor to Him whom we love.

Acknowledgments

Some debts you can't wait to pay—such as the debt of gratitude owed to those who made this book possible.

Carolyn McCready, Harvest House Publishers VP of Editorial— Thank you for easing my worries as I struggled with a looming deadline and a creative spirit crushed by the events of 9/11. Truly, the kindness and understanding you expressed was a balm of healing to this author's soul.

Harvest House publicists, marketing mavens, and sales reps— You are simply indispensable! Your individual attention to detail as well as your collective enthusiasm for the books I've written is a key factor in their success. It's a joy to work with such wonderful men and women!

Chip MacGregor, literary agent par excellence—You make me laugh, "get" my oddball humor, and let me talk through (endlessly it seems!) the ideas, the projects, and the desires of my writing soul. Not only are you an agent/business partner but a friend—a brother in Christ who continues to sharpen my faith and encourages me to dream big.

Paul Gossard, manuscript editor—for dotting the i's, crossing the t's, and helping me grasp the use of brackets for interpolations of material into quotations! It is a compassionate editor indeed who asks, "Could you flesh out chapter 6 just a bit?" when that chapter in fact consists of two pages!

Rachel St. John Gilbert—With one insightful e-mail you pulled together the pieces of a disjointed book idea and introduction. Your ability to see the details in my concept helped set my fingers to typing!

Mom and Dad—You've loved me in spite of my financial mismanagement and have always, always, always been there for Rick and me. If I can't repay you with money, let me do so with love and thanks.

Rod and Dona Barnhill, brother- and sister-in-law—We've been there for each other for close to 15 years now. I think we took the vows with you guys too! No matter how gloomy the financial report has looked, you've remained right by our side.

Rick Barnhill, husband and co–financial loser—For better, for worse, for richer, for poorer, 'til death do us part. I love you.

Appendix:
Recommended Reading and Other Helpful Resources

You're going to enjoy reading and exploring the various sources offered in this appendix.

I've paid careful attention to suggest only those books, guides, and online sites that offer *practical* help for finances and marriage. If you're an Internet lover you'll want to pay careful attention to the dot-coms listed for each—and as any Web surfer knows, there are hundreds of other valuable sites to be found. Just use google.com, type in your keywords, and enjoy! And since we *are* in financial straits, please don't overlook the free and friendly services available at your local public library, which enable you to get online or take home a great book at no cost.

Money-and-Marriage Reality

IVillage Moneylife. Access <http://www.quiz.ivillage.com/money life/tests/personality.htm>.
Take this quiz and learn how your individual qualities affect your money life.

Warren, Neil. *God Said It, Don't Sweat It: How to Keep Life's Petty Hassles from Overwhelming You.* Nashville, TN: Thomas Nelson, 1998.

Wright, Dr. H. Norman. "Money and Your Marriage—Blessing or Curse?" <http://www.christianity.com/CC/article/0,,PTID1000| CHID74|CIID324527,00.html >. Accessed December 2001.

Realistic Expectations

Arterburn, Stephen, Fred Stoeker, and Mike Yorkey. *Every Woman's Desire: An Every Man's Guide to Winning the Heart of a Woman.* Colorado Springs, CO: Waterbrook Press, 2001.

Chapman, Dr. Gary. *The Five Love Languages: How to Express Heartfelt Commitment to Your Mate.* Chicago: Northfield Publishers, 1992.

Gibson, Roger C. *First Comes Love, Then Comes Money: Basic Steps to Avoid the #1 Conflict in Marriage.* Green Forest, AR: New Leaf Press, 1998.

Thurman, Dr. Chris. *The Lies We Believe.* Nashville, TN: Thomas Nelson, 1991.
Superb look at the lies we believe as married couples.

Truthful Communications

Barrington, Alan D., "He Said, She Said," online article: <http://www. christianitytoday.com/mp/8m1/8m1012.html>.
I read this short article and loved it! See—we're not the only ones having a difficult time communicating!

Foster, Dr. Charles. *There's Something I Have to Tell You: How to Communicate Difficult News in Tough Situations.* New York: Harmony Books, 1997.

Vernick, Leslie. *Acting Right When Your Spouse Acts Wrong.* Colorado Springs, CO: Waterbrook Press, 2001.

Contentment

Alcorn, Randy C. *Money, Possessions and Eternity.* Wheaton, IL: Tyndale House Publishers, Inc., 1989.

Brooks, Bobbe. "Trusting God, Not Credit Cards." Online article: <http://www.christianwomentoday.com/money/creditcard.html>.

Callaway, Phil. *Making Life Rich Without Any Money.* Eugene, OR: Harvest House Publishers, 1998.

Dillow, Linda. *Calm My Anxious Heart: A Woman's Guide to Contentment.* Colorado Springs, CO: NavPress, 1998.

Fryling, Alice. *Reshaping a Jealous Heart: How to Turn Dissatisfaction into Contentment.* Downer's Grove, IL: InterVarsity Press, 1994. *While this is listed as out of print at Amazon.com, there are used books available to purchase. Well worth it!*

Ramsey, Dave. *Financial Peace: Restoring Hope to You and Your Family.* New York: Viking, 1997.

Wiersbe, Warren. *Be Satisfied.* Colorado Springs, CO: Chariot Victor Books, 1990.

No Regrets

Arthur, Kay. *A Marriage Without Regrets.* Eugene, OR: Harvest House Publishers, 2000.

Wilkerson, Susan. *Getting Past Your Past: Finding Freedom from the Pain of Regret.* Sisters, OR: Multnomah Publishers, 2000.

Staying in Your Marriage

Chapman, Dr. Gary. *Toward a Growing Marriage: Building the Love Relationship of Your Dreams.* Chicago: Moody Press, 1996.

Fuller, Cheri. *When Couples Pray.* Sisters, OR: Multnomah Publishers, 2001.

Gottman, John, PhD, and Nancy Glass. *Why Marriages Succeed or Fail: And How You Can Make Yours Last.* New York: Simon & Schuster, 1994.

Smalley, Gary. *Winning Your Wife Back Before It's Too Late: Whether She's Left Physically or Emotionally.* Nashville, TN: Thomas Nelson, 1999. *The author also has another book, titled* Winning Your Husband Back Before It's Too Late. *Each one speaks to the heart and gives practical information for your marriage's success.*

Weiner, Michele Davis. *Divorce Busting: A Revolutionary and Rapid Program for Staying Together.* Fireside, 1993.
Straightforward advice and encouragement for hanging in there with one another!

Wheat, Ed, and Gloria Okes Perkins. *Staying in Love for a Lifetime: Love Life for Every Married Couple; The 1st Years of Forever; Secret Choices.* Budget Book Service, 1999.

Online Marriage Resources

The Center for Marriage and Family Studies: <http://www.life relationships.org/>. Mission statement: "The mission of the Center is to have a major impact on marriages and families by providing Christ-centered education and intervention."
You'll enjoy the wide range of content and practical tools for building a healthy and strong marriage.

Covenant Keepers: <http://www.covenantkeepers.org/index.html>. Mission Statement: "We believe that God's Word supplies all the answers needed to enable a loving relationship that glorifies God. Through our quarterly publication of Covenant Keepers we strengthen the Biblical approach to counseling marriages. Through seminars and workshops, we provide the Body of Christ with the principles and practical application of God's Word for marriage."

Smalleyonline.com: <http://smalley.gospelcom.net/>. Mission statement: "The Smalley Relationship Center's mission is to rebuild, restore and renew marriages that have been devastated for generations. We want to accomplish this by reducing divorce and raising marital satisfaction for every couple!"
Yet another terrific site for those wanting online information!

Online Financial Information & Resources

Barnabas Financial Ministry: <http://www.barnabasministry.org.> Mission statement: "We serve the church community by communicating Biblical truths that lead to true, personal, financial freedom. Using seminars, media, public speaking, teacher/counselor training, materials, networking and individual counseling, we provide information, hope and encouragement that helps people out of financial bondage, setting them free to give their time and resources to God's work."

Christian Money.com: <http://www.christianmoney.com>.
Lots and lots of advice from easy to understand financial wizard Jim Paris. You'll like this site and enjoy dipping into all the information he provides.

Credit reports: *If you're wondering how to get your consolidated credit report,* visit <http://www.truecredit.com>.
Many companies offer consolidated or "three-bureau" credit reports, but "truecredit" is the report recommended by the nonprofit financial crisis center www.myvesta.org.

Crown Financial Ministries: "Teaching People God's Financial Principles." Online article: <http:///www.crown.org>.
There is a little bit of everything at this marvelous site, from online tools to radio broadcast archives; you'll find what you need.

Financial Planning: <http://financialplan.about.com/cs/familyfinances/index_2.htm>.
I like to browse through this site's various articles regarding money and relationships.

Financial Advice Books

Hayden, Ruth L. *For Richer, Not Poorer—The Money Book for Couples.* Deerfield Beach, FL: Health Communications, 1999.

Hunt, Mary. *The Financially Confident Woman.* Nashville, TN: Broadman and Holman Publishers, 1996.

McNaughton, Deborah. *All About Credit: Questions (and Answers) About the Most Common Credit Problems.* Chicago: Dearborn Trade Publishing, 1999.

Budgeting 101 Books

Kay, Ellie. *Shop, Save, and Share.* Minneapolis: Bethany House, 1998.

Sander, Peter J., and Jennifer Bayse Sander. *The Pocket Idiot's Guide to Living on a Budget.* Alpha Books, 1999.

Grace-Filled Books for Living

Callaway, Phil. *Who Put the Skunk in the Trunk?: Learning to Laugh When Life Stinks.* Sisters, OR: Multnomah Publishers, 2000.

I like this comparison that I read at www.amazon.com: "Callaway's book is a more practical version of works like Philip Yancey's Where is God When It Hurts *or Harold Kushner's* When Bad Things Happen to Good People. *Callaway does not try to explain the mystery of human suffering. Instead, he tells dozens of stories of people rising above their suffering with faith and laughter." I would agree. Phil's practical yet profound philosophy speaks straight to the frustrated and hurting soul.*

Foster, Richard J. *The Challenge of the Disciplined Life: Christian Reflections on Money, Sex & Power.* San Francisco: HarperSanFrancisco, 1999.

Lamott, Anne. *Traveling Mercies: Some Thoughts on Faith.* New York: Anchor Books, 1999.

Please note: Anne Lamott is not for the faint-of-heart. However, her stories and observations testify to this marvelous truth: God's grace extends to misfits of every stripe.

Manning, Brennan. *The Ragamuffin Gospel.* Sisters, OR: Multnomah Publishers, 2000.

One of my absolute favorite books of all time!

Yancey, Philip. *What's So Amazing About Grace?* Grand Rapids, MI: Zondervan Publishing House, 1997.

Notes

1. Inspired by a phrase from a speech by Sir Winston Churchill, "Never give in, never, never, never," as found at <http:www.winston churchill.org/speeches.htm>: "Complete Speeches of Winston Churchill." October 29, 1941, Harrow School; Accessed August 2001.

2. Brennan Manning, *The Ragamuffin Gospel* (Sisters, OR: Mult-nomah Publishers, 2000), p. 166.

3. Olivia Mellan, *Money Harmony: Resolving Money Conflicts in Your Life and Relationships*, p. 30.

4. Dave Meurer, *Daze of Our Wives: A Semi-Helpful Guide to Marital Bliss* (Minneapolis: Bethany House Publishers, 2000), pp. 23-24.

5. Les Parrott III, *Saving Your Marriage Before It Starts* (Grand Rapids, MI: Zondervan, 1995), p. 84.

6. Adapted from the *Family Digest* article "The Stages of Marriage: A Roadmap to Marital Bliss" by Darryl E. Owens. Found at <http://www.familydigest.com/stories/marriagestages.cfm>. Accessed December 2001.

7. Louise Lague, "How Honest Are Couples, Really?" *Readers Digest*, August 2001, pp. 91-92.

8. "The Solid Rock," words by Edward Mote (1834).

9. M.P. Dunleavey, "The Hidden Costs of Too Much Stuff," found at <http://moneycentral.msn.com/articles/smartbuy/basics/7401.asp>. Accessed September 2001.

10. Adapted from *She's Gonna Blow: Real Help for Moms Dealing with Anger* (Eugene, OR: Harvest House Publishers, 2001), pp. 82-84.

11. Geoff Sparkes and Annette Hall, found at Oceans Enterprise Website, <http://www.oceans.com.au/oefun-100people.html>. Accessed October 2001.

12. "I Still Do," a marriage conference provided through the ministry of FamilyLife. Led by radio host and author/speaker Dennis Rainey. Further information can be found at <http://www.istilldo.com>.

13. Dennis Rainey, "Love for a Lifetime," online interview with Holly J. Lebowitz, found at Beliefnet, www.beliefnet.org/story51/story_5160_l.html. Accessed October 2001.

14. Brennan Manning, *Reflections for Ragamuffins* (San Francisco: HarperSanFrancisco, 1998), p. 230.

15. Matthew Henry, "I Corinthians 13:4," *Complete Commentary on the Whole Bible,* originally published 1706, reprinted online at Crosswalk.com: <bible.crosswalk.com/Commentaries/Matthew HenryComplete/mhc-com>. Accessed January 2002.

16. Henry.

17. Source unknown.

18. As found in Mary Batchelor, compiler, *Poetry for the Soul* (Nashville, TN: Moorings, 1995), p. 410.

19. Manning, *Reflections for Ragamuffins,* p. 230.

You can visit Julie Barnhill's Web site at:
<www.juliebarnhill.com>

If you are interested in having Julie Ann Barnhill
speak at your special event, please contact:

Speak Up Speaker Services
1614 Edison Shores Place
Port Huron, MI 48060-3374
Voice: 810-982-0898
Fax: 810-987-4163
E-mail: speakupinc@aol.com

Or log on to <www.speakupspeakerservices.com>
for online scheduling

"You'll laugh, you'll cry, and you'll identify
with Julie's open, honest approach."

Gary Chapman, PhD,
author of *The Five Love Languages of Children*

"To every mother who's ever blown it, yelled when she should
have sent herself to time-out, and wants to believe she can
change—this book is for you."

Becky Freeman,
national speaker and author of *Chocolate Chili Pepper Love* and *Peanut Butter
Kisses and Mud Pie Hugs*

"Look Out—She's Gonna Blow!"

Yes, you *do* love your kids—and other moms struggle with feelings of anger just like you do!

A "been-there-done-that" mom herself, Julie Barnhill turns the hilarious scenes of everyday life with kids into a practical guide for anyone who's wrestling with the down-to-earth realities of being a mom. If you've ever experienced the following...

- You were going to be a "good mother"—but it only worked until the kids were born

- You find yourself saying "never again," and then blowing it yet another time

- You get to the end of the day and realize you haven't laughed, relaxed, or enjoyed your children

...*She's Gonna Blow!* will offer you hope, honest understanding, and good measures of laughter and wise biblical counsel. Julie will help show you the way back to the God who knows your mother heart as no one else does—and who offers lifelong peace and change for your journey of mothering!

Other Books About Money and Marriage from Harvest House

I Love You, But Why Are We So Different?
Tim LaHaye

Giving you hands-on tools for turning personal differences into marriage-enriching experiences, Tim LaHaye, who has sold more than 8 million nonfiction books, helps you and your spouse understand your strengths and weaknesses, and offers steps to build a dynamic relationship.

Money Management for Those Who Don't Have Any
James L. Paris

If your financial problems need solutions fast, this guide will provide it, with over 200 strategies for budgeting, reducing expenses, borrowing wisely, lowering insurance fees and taxes, and even having fun without "fun" money.

Chocolate Chili Pepper Love
Becky Freeman

Finding humor and hope amid the clutter of kids and romantic moments gone wrong, Becky celebrates the journey of marriage, including the easy "vanilla" marriages, fun "strawberry" marriages, and exciting "chocolate chili pepper" marriages.

Men Are Like Waffles, Women Are Like Spaghetti
Bill and Pam Farrel

Men keep life elements in separate boxes; women intertwine everything. Providing biblical insights, sound research, and humorous anecdotes, the Farrels explore gender differences and preferences and how they can strengthen relationships.

A Marriage Without Regrets
Kay Arthur

Speaking candidly about her failed first marriage, her conversion to Christianity, and her current marriage, Kay offers practical, biblical advice on communication, significance, and parenting. She also covers God's guidelines for divorce and remarriage. Also available as an audiobook.